Camino de Santiago

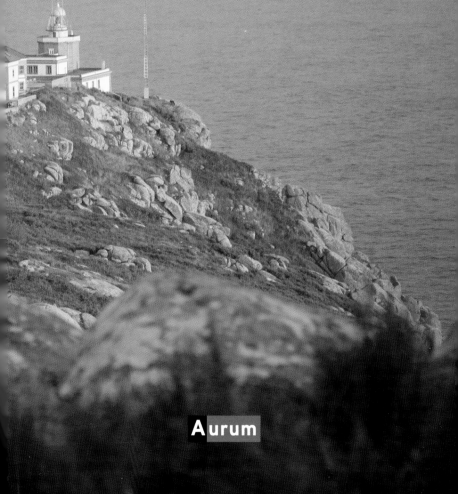

Camino de Santiago

**The ancient Way of Saint James pilgrimage route from
the French Pyrenees to Santiago de Compostela**

Sergi Ramis

Translated by Peter Barraclough

Aurum

First published in English in a fully revised and updated edition 2012 by
Aurum Press Ltd
7 Greenland Street
London NW1 0ND
www.aurumpress.co.uk

Published by arrangement with Ecos Producciones Periodisticas, SCP

ISBN 978 1 84513 708 3

10 9 8 7 6 5 4 3 2 1
2016 2015 2014 2013 2012

Text design by Xavier Peralta
Typeset in Rotis Serif by MRules
Printed in China

Aurum Press want to ensure that these Trail Guides are always as up to date as possible –
but stiles collapse, pubs close and bus services change all the time. If, on walking this path,
you discover any important changes that future walkers need to be aware of, do let us know.
Either email us on trailguides@aurumpress.co.uk with your comments, or if you take the
trouble to drop us a line to:
Trail Guides, Aurum Press, 7 Greenland Street, London NW1 0ND,
we'll send you a free guide of your choice as thanks.

Contents

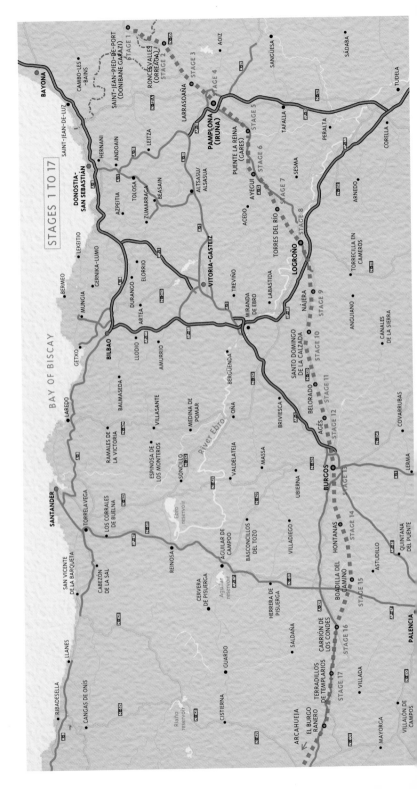

STAGES 1 TO 17

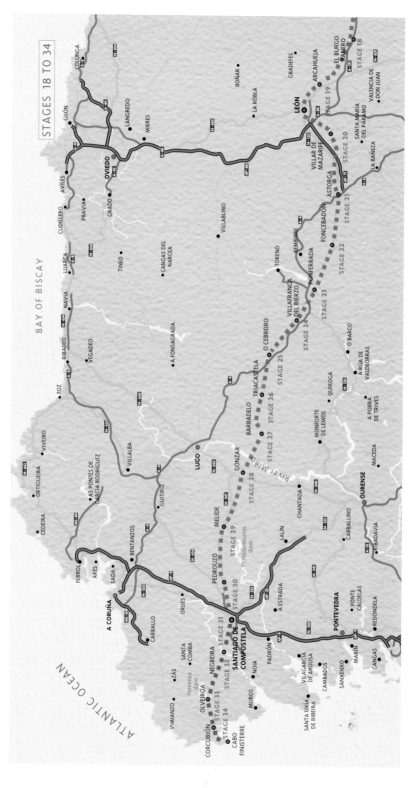

STAGES 18 TO 34

BAY OF BISCAY

ATLANTIC OCEAN

COLUNGA
GIJÓN
AVILÉS
CUDILLERO
PRAVIA
LUARCA
NAVIA
RIBADEO
VEGADEO
FOZ
VIVEIRO
ORTIGUEIRA
CEDEIRA
FERROL
ARES
SADA
A CORUÑA
CARBALLO
ORDES
SANTA COMBA
ZÁS
VIMIANZO
MUROS
NOIA
PADRÓN
A ESTRADA
LALÍN
CHANTADA
VILAGARCÍA DE AROUSA
SANTA UXÍA DE RIBEIRA
CAMBADOS
SANXENXO
MARÍN
CANGAS
PONTEVEDRA
PONTE CALDELAS
REDONDELA
RIBADAVIA
CARBALLINO
OURENSE
MACEDA
A POBRA DE TRIVES
MONFORTE DE LEMOS
QUIROGA
A RÚA DE VALDEORRAS
O BARCO
PONFERRADA
TORENO
VILLABLINO
CANGAS DEL NARCEA
TINEO
A FONSAGRADA
VILLALBA
AS PONTES DE GARCÍA RODRÍGUEZ
GUITIRIZ
LUGO
MELIDE
GONZAR
BARBADELO
TRIACASTELA
O CEBREIRO
VILLAFRANCA DEL BIERZO
BEMBIBRE
ASTORGA
FONCEBADÓN
LA BAÑEZA
SANTA MARÍA DEL PÁRAMO
VILLAR DE MAZARIFE
LEÓN
ARCAHUEJA
EL BURGO RANERO
VALENCIA DE DON JUAN
GRADEFES
BOÑAR
LA ROBLA
LANGREDO
MIERES
OVIEDO
GRADO

Portodemouros dam
Fervenza dam
RIVER MIÑO

PEDROUZO
NEGREIRA
SANTIAGO DE COMPOSTELA
OLVEIROA
CORCUBIÓN
CABO FINISTERRE

STAGE 18
STAGE 19
STAGE 20
STAGE 21
STAGE 22
STAGE 23
STAGE 24
STAGE 25
STAGE 26
STAGE 27
STAGE 28
STAGE 29
STAGE 30
STAGE 31
STAGE 32
STAGE 33
STAGE 34

The Way as it is **today**

From the standpoint of the number of pilgrims recorded, *el Camino de Santiago* (the Way of Saint James) is currently reliving the golden age of over a thousand years ago, when, with the support of the authorities, this route was opened up to everyone.

These days pilgrims choose to walk the Way for many reasons: sport, tourism or the thirst for new experience run side by side with religious motivation. The pilgrims who set out for Santiago de Compostela do not always do so for devotional reasons, but they soon discover that they are on a journey not only across the north of the Iberian Peninsula but also into the depths of their own minds. In the course of that journey they will have the opportunity to visit some of the most impressive cathedrals in Spain, together with small villages whose names they had never heard before, and will come into contact with other people from all over the world. However, their physical and mental endurance will also be tested. The Way of Saint James is many journeys in one.

The pilgrimage need no longer be devotional, but it rapidly becomes an introspective journey

Every year over 100,000 people undertake the pilgrimage to Santiago de Compostela, starting out from different points. The summer months remain by far the most popular, accounting for more than 60% of the travellers. There are still improvements to be made: the signs, for example, could be a little more uniform and if more amenities remained open in the low season there might be a better spread of pilgrims throughout the year. It would also be great if something could be done about the conmen who try to take advantage of pilgrims. However, since they too have been around for a thousand years, that might prove impossible.

Despite the need for changes, the Way is still an amazing journey, on which pilgrims discover as much about themselves as they do about the country they are walking through. Benefiting from the different perspective provided by a journey on foot, they more fully appreciate the architecture and landscape, while coming into contact with different people, cultures and languages. There is, furthermore, the sensation of spiritual purity, of being free from sin, if only for a day.

Preparing for the journey

It is essential to select the route you are going to follow and determine the distance you intend to cover. According to the records kept by the ecclesiastical authorities of Santiago de Compostela, every year some 100,000 pilgrims claim, upon their arrival in the city, the *compostela*, a certificate to show that they have travelled at least 100 km of the Way on foot, by bicycle or on horseback. August, July, June and September, in that order, are the months in which most of them arrive. During the rest of the year the Way is considerably quieter. However, comparatively few of those pilgrims make the whole of the journey from the classic starting points of Saint-Jean-Pied-de-Port (in Basque: Donibane Garazi) or Roncesvalles (in Basque: Orreaga). Many more choose to start out from some intermediate point, such as Burgos or León, while a vast number cover the Galician section alone, beginning either at O Cebreiro, the point of entry into the autonomous

community of Galicia, or at Sarria, which is just far enough from Santiago de Compostela to provide the 100 km distance required for the *compostela*.

The Way in fact comprises various paths starting in different places. This guide focuses on the *Camino Francés* (the French Way) right from its starting point on the French side of the Pyrenees. Bear in mind, however, that in practice the route may be shortened; the information provided is organized in convenient stages.

From that starting point the distance to be covered is close to

700 km and the journey, on foot, may take over four weeks. In light of this it is worth considering the following factors.

Dates and stages

According to statistics, more than half of pilgrims are Spanish. This helps to explain why the greatest number of travellers come in the summer months, as it is then that holidays are traditionally taken in Spain. However, while June and September are very good months for undertaking a journey of this nature, July and August, unfortunately, are not. Obviously at that time of year, the traveller has the advantage of many hours of daylight, but there are also serious disadvantages: the temperature tends to be very high, even from the early morning, the sun is equally strong and the amenities are crowded. As a result, in recent years pilgrims have practically been forced to engage in

a race to see who starts the day earliest, completes the stage first and so manages to get a place at the next hostel. This is contrary to the very nature of the pilgrimage, which calls for calm, a measured pace and time in which to visit the places of interest along the way. If the journey becomes little more than a continuation of everyday stress, you are going to achieve very little.

The best seasons in which to undertake the pilgrimage are without doubt spring and autumn. Most of the hostels are open and the temperature is usually pleasant, while the days are sufficiently long to allay the fear of still being outside when night falls. Only rain and the occasional flurry of snow test the resistance of the traveller.

Winter is only for the hardy. Although ideal for those who are mentally and physically strong, a winter's journey entails crossing the Pyrenees at the toughest time, enduring the biting winds and low

temperatures of Castilla y León and withstanding the rains of El Bierzo and Galicia. Furthermore, many hostels, restaurants and bars are closed at this time of year. Careful planning is therefore required if travellers are not to find themselves without accommodation at the end of a hard day's walk.

After deciding on the starting date, the next step is to determine, with care, how long the various stages should be. This guide includes none surpassing 30 km in a day. Although we may hear other pilgrims boast of having walked 35, 40 or 45 km in that time, this is not something that we would reco-mmend. The journey should above all be pleasant. Time should be allowed to visit villages, churches and bridges, to take refreshment in a bar, to have a picnic in a meadow.

It is also necessary to consider the potentially adverse effects of long sustained effort.

Among hikers it is customary to measure distances in terms of hours rather than kilometres. In this guide we have therefore given preference to this means of estimating what can be done in a day, as we find it more logical. However, as the 'tradition' of the Way requires that distances also be indicated in kilometres, we have provided this form of measurement as well. We obtained it using a personal pedometer, although these devices are not particularly precise, as everyone knows, and the results they yield depend on the length of each individual's stride. It is therefore better to be guided by the hours and minutes mentioned in each case, as these indications are

Physical preparation

People of all ages can easily take on the task of walking the Way of Saint James provided that they are in good physical condition. Except for the first stage and for a few later stretches (reached when the body has become accustomed to the effort), most of the route is gentle or with climbs of little difficulty. The aim is to walk for four to six hours a day on average, something that is within anyone's capacity. However, it is the overall duration of the journey that may give rise to problems.

While it is true that everyone should be able to walk for various hours a day, even without preparation, it does not follow that everyone can maintain that rhythm for a month. The muscles will suffer and send out signals in the form of stiffness or pain. Worse still, a case of tendonitis may send us straight home. For these reasons it is particularly important to train a little during the weeks preceding the journey in order to tone up the body.

Mental preparation

A few pilgrims are experienced hikers or fell-walkers accustomed to making long journeys on foot. The others may be well advised to undertake a little mental preparation for the experience by taking the following points on board.

• Your feet will be the means of transport, so walk at your own speed, neither faster nor slower than the body dictates.

• Local people are generally friendly and even affectionate towards pilgrims. However, you will also come across those prepared to take advantage of the vulnerability of the traveller on foot looking for a place to sleep and a meal.

• The hostels are not hotels but just lodging places. The facilities may often be very basic or poorly maintained.

• Many *hospitaleros* (hospitallers: those who receive the pilgrims and help out at the hostels) are unpaid volunteers. Try to make their work easier rather than more difficult by being polite and grateful.

• There are days when the wind, the heat, the cold, the rain or the snow will put a strain on your nervous system. Try to be positive and assertive in the face of these difficulties and don't let the problem get on top of you.

much more reliable and provide the walker with references that are easier to follow.

The signs along the Way

Signs bearing the characteristic yellow arrows have been erected all along the Way by the owners of hostels, town councils, the autonomous communities or the associations of friends of the Way of Saint James. The route is therefore marked from start to finish. There are, however, still some stretches where the marking is not entirely clear. If you encounter this problem it is always better to ask a local for assistance rather than walking on in the direction you think is right. What's more, this guide provides all

Gear

Although the Way runs through parts of the Iberian Peninsula which have not developed any real tourist industry, all the services you are going to require are available. The pilgrim need therefore only prepare the lightest possible backpack. If it weighs more than 10 kilos, you have already made your first mistake. The well-prepared backpack should have a capacity of no more than 35 litres and contain:

- A sleeping bag.
- A minimum amount of clothing (most hostels have a washing machine and drier).
- Flip-flops for the shower and for resting the feet.
- A towel.
- A small toilet bag.
- A small first aid kit.
- Basic rain and wind gear.
- A water bottle.
- Sunglasses and sun cream.
- A hat or cap.
- A guidebook, necessary documents, money and a camera.

Subsequent needs that might arise can be dealt with in the course of the journey. There should be no difficulty in obtaining, for example, a given medicine, additional warm clothing, lip balm, moist tissues, etc., especially since the Way crosses cities of a certain size, such as Pamplona, Logroño, Burgos and León.

the necessary help for negotiating places where the lack of signs or, at times, the abundance of them could give rise to confusion.

On the Way, looking after the body
On a long journey like this it is important that you are well aware, at all times, that your body is your means of transport. You should therefore be sure to provide it with every possible care so that it may withstand the effort.

It is best to get up early and start out at about eight o'clock, although in the summer an hour earlier, when day will already have broken, is an even better time. You will thus have the advantage of being able to walk for three or four hours before the heat sets in.

It is advisable to eat a full breakfast and, once on the path, to take a pause and have a drink of water every hour or so. Some prefer an isotonic drink in order to replace salts, but be warned, especially if you need to watch your sugar levels, that these drinks contain a lot of it.

Lunch is best kept light but should naturally provide energy. A sandwich, dried fruits and nuts, fresh fruit or an energy bar will suffice and not sit heavily on the stomach when you take to the path once again with a view to concluding the day's walk in the early afternoon. You can then have a snack and, later, a hearty hot dinner, although even then you should avoid food that is excessively heavy or greasy as it could prevent you from sleeping well.

Alcohol not only impairs your

attentiveness but also dehydrates the body. Pilgrims should therefore keep their alcohol intake to a minimum. Although in the heat of midday or at the end of a stage you may feel that you have 'earned' a beer, it is wise to exercise moderation.

It is important to sleep well and for an appropriate number of hours. On the Way you will meet

many other people and the temptation to stay up talking until late is evident. However, the body needs at least eight hours' rest in order to recover from the efforts of the day and be ready to meet the next challenge.

You should above all look after your feet, as they are your 'engine'. Comfortable, well-used trekking or hiking boots, with a good sole, are the appropriate footwear. Socks should never wrinkle or bunch. There are socks for hikers which have reinforced toes, soles and heels designed specifically to guard against that risk. While there are also traditional remedies for the much feared chafes or blisters, sticking on a strip of artificial skin, available at all chemists, may be the best solution. The pain disappears almost instantly and the dressing remains adhered until the wound heals.

Life at the hostels

As we have already said, the hostels are not hotels. They are modestly priced for a reason: you will be sharing rooms and facilities. It is therefore important to make an orderly use of the allotted space, to help ensure that the bathrooms and common areas do not get too dirty, to leave the kitchen clean after use and to take the maximum care not to disturb the sleep of others. Unfortunately, snorers can prove a nightmare, although the number of hostels providing separate dormitories to group them apart is constantly increasing. It is therefore by no means a bad idea to carry earplugs, as they are the most effective solution.

Some hostels offer dinners. Haute cuisine it is not, but the dishes are energy-giving and filling. Where that service is not available, there are bars and restaurants in the vicinity which will generally give set meals at special prices for pilgrims.

To have the right to use the state-run hostels and also some of the private ones (although at others no questions are asked) the pilgrim must be in possession of a *credencial*. This is a pilgrim's pass obtainable at the offices of the association of friends of the Way of Saint James in Galicia and at some churches. It is also important to remember that this document must be stamped upon the completion of each stage and shown at the Pilgrim's Office in Santiago if you want to obtain the *compostela* at the end of your journey.

Precautions on the Way

The French Way is very well kept and pilgrims rarely have to walk unprotected on the hard shoulder of a road. However, there are some such stretches and on those you will need to concentrate. It is best to walk on the left, facing the oncoming traffic. In the dark wear brightly coloured clothes and carry a torch so that drivers can see you are there. It is, of course, important to take great care when crossing roads or railway lines. You will sometimes see memorials commemorating pilgrims who died as a result of their own carelessness, or because of someone else's. If you are careful you won't add to their number!

The Way is, in general, safe from a personal standpoint, although some women have reported being attacked or molested at given places and times. In the hostels it is advisable to keep an eye on personal belongings, money and valuables, such as cameras and jewellery.

On the Way, moments of fatigue

As there are pilgrims of all ages and physical conditions, various help

On the Way, avoid giving offence

Many of the places through which the pilgrim passes are not set up for tourists. So try to respect local traditions: remove headgear when entering a church, dress with reasonable decorum and refrain from bathing nude in lakes or rivers if local people take umbrage. Your aim should be to relate to others without causing offence either to their eyes or to their way of thinking, irrespective of your personal opinions or beliefs.

services, which can prove very useful, have sprung up along the Way. One of these is backpack carriage. It is provided by taxis which will take your pack to the place you name, although not always for a modest charge. It can certainly prove practical if you happen not to be feeling too well or are suffering from momentary muscular pain. This service tends to be very popular on stages like that from Villafranca del Bierzo to O Cebreiro, where travellers face a stiff climb lasting for some hours.

THE PILGRIMAGE **BY BIKE**

To travel the Way of Saint James by bicycle is easy. Indeed, it might almost be termed relaxing. All the recommendations given in the preceding pages concerning equipment, nourishment, rest and behaviour are similarly valid for cyclists. However, cyclists should also give consideration to certain additional factors relating specifically to their chosen means of transport.

The bike

It is possible to cover the whole of the French Way by road. To do so, however, is not only dangerous but also boring. It is better to follow the yellow arrows and to pedal along tracks, unmade roads, paved ways and, on a few occasion, narrow paths. When this second course is chosen, the bike needs to be versatile with a robust frame. Mixed-surface tyres are the best for this varied terrain. There is no need for mountain bike tyres, which have a lot of grip and are slow, while road tyres would without doubt suffer frequent punctures.

Gear

Given the speeds they reach, cyclists may feel the cold more acutely than walkers, especially on rainy or snowy days. It is advisable to bear this in mind when packing. While the weight to be carried should always be kept as low as possible, it is important to ensure that the hands and feet will be adequately protected, as those are the parts of the cyclist which suffer most.

The bicycle, not the cyclist, should carry the gear. The bike should therefore be equipped with waterproof pannier bags and everything that has to be carried should be stowed in these or fastened to the luggage rack. It is not advisable for cyclists to carry a backpack, however small, as it will

tire them and impede their natural movement on the bike, above all on uphill stretches.

In addition to the standard gear, cyclists should carry a basic repair kit comprising spare tubes, puncture patches, a chain tool, a screwdriver and a multi-purpose wrench. Many towns along the Way have garages that work specifically with bicycles. If one of these is not to be found, however, any other garage dealing with cars or motorbikes may be able to help out.

It is also a good idea to carry a decent lock for use when there is no place for the bike inside the hostel.

The stages

In a day the average cyclist can easily cover three times the distance walked by a pilgrim on foot. To plan to complete the journey in ten days (see page 17) is therefore by no means unrealistic. However, it is necessary to bear in mind that adverse circumstances may be encountered. There is, for example, the wind, which can be very strong on the northern plain and tends to blow from the west. It is therefore in the pilgrim's face.

The guidelines previously provided about what to expect and how to behave at hostels apply to cyclists too. In their case, however, it is also important to remember that the wheels of their bike may be dirty. Consequently, for the same reason that at many hostels pilgrims are required to remove their boots before setting foot on the facilities, cyclists should take care that their bicycles are not trailing mud and leaves into the building.

Many hostels have parking facilities or areas where bikes may safely be left for the night. Others, however, do not have space enough and there is consequently no option but to leave the bike in the street. When that is the case any loose parts which may be stolen should first be removed, as the next morning you might otherwise find yourselves without the means to continue the journey.

The first stage, a test

As it starts out from Saint-Jean-Pied-de-Port (in Basque: Donibane Garazi), the first stage of the French Way puts the pilgrim to the test. If it is hard for the walker, it can be tougher still for the cyclist. So be wary of overconfidence and warm up well before starting. The route is steeply uphill from the outset and remains thus almost until you reach the Ibañeta pass. To start out cold could therefore result in muscular injury and put a very early end to the journey.

The best plan is first to spend half an hour pedalling along the flat terrain in the valley in order to work up a sweat. Then, when the muscles of the legs and arms have warmed up, you will be in better shape to take on the tough climb over the Pyrenees.

You should take great care when subsequently riding down into Roncesvalles (Orreaga) and, for that matter, on all the other downhill stretches along the Way. You may encounter other pilgrims on foot, local people doing agricultural work, flocks of sheep, herds of cows, or simply other vehicles. Breakneck descents are therefore never a good idea. Make sure your brakes are in good working order and be ready to use them at all times.

The advantages of the cyclist

It can be extremely hard for a walker, upon reaching the end of a stage, tired out, to be told that the hostel is full and that the next one is three kilometres away. For the cyclist it is much less so. That said, cyclists should plan their stages in such a way that an unexpected extension does not tax them to the limit. Stages of 60 or 70 km are therefore to be recommended. After a stage of 100 km or more, they may find it difficult to cope with an unforeseen circumstance of this kind.

The Way in 10 days

The Way at a **glance**

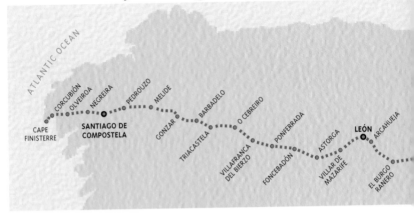

ATLANTIC OCEAN

CAPE FINISTERRE — CORCUBIÓN — OLVEIROA — NEGREIRA — SANTIAGO DE COMPOSTELA — PEDROUZO — MELIDE — GONZAR — BARBADELO — TRIACASTELA — O CEBREIRO — VILLAFRANCA DEL BIERZO — PONFERRADA — FONCEBADÓN — ASTORGA — VILLAR DE MAZARIFE — LEÓN — ARCAHUEJA — EL BURGO RANERO

Lower Navarre

The Way commences in, and passes briefly through, Lower Navarre on the north side of the Pyrenees. This stage is intense, comprising the steep climb over the Pyrenees and the descent on the other side. The architectural highlight is the walled town of Saint-Jean-Pied-de-Port (Donibane Garazi).

The pass over the Pyrenees, at the very beginning of the Way, is one of the most physically demanding stretches (→ STAGE 1, page 26)

Estella (Lizarra) is one of the most important Navarran towns on the Way (→ STAGE 5, page 48)

Navarre

The capital of Navarre, Pamplona (Iruña), is the first city that the pilgrims cross. They also pass through towns of great historic importance for the pilgrimage, such as Estella and Puente la Reina. The mountains now lie behind and rolling countryside, dotted with vineyards, opens up. The Way is heading west.

La Rioja

The Way crosses the north part of La Rioja. Although

flanked by mountains, it runs along the valley floor. In this region you will find such jewels of religious architecture as the monastery of Santa María la Real in Nájera, or the harmonious urban setting of Santo Domingo de la

The Pilgrims' Fountain in Logroño, a boon to the traveller (→ STAGE 8, page 62)

Calzada, associated with the famous legend of the cock and hen that crowed after having been roasted.

Castilla y León

Here you find the historic cities of Burgos and León,

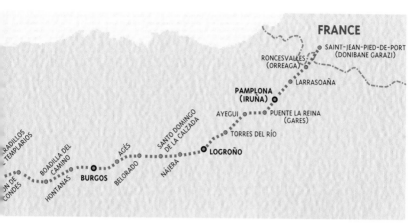

Stained-glass windows in the cathedral of León, a masterpiece of Gothic architecture
(→ STAGE 19, page 114)

with their great cathedrals, but also the taxing plain of Palencia. This is a stiff test for the foot pilgrim, who has to walk for the space of two weeks through a never-ending plain of cornfields with few visual references.

Galicia

Upon setting foot on Galician soil the pilgrim has the feeling that the journey's end is near, although there is

in fact still a week remaining. That week may, however, ultimately seem to go by all too soon, as this is the land of corredoiras (the ancient paths linking the villages), chestnut woods, farming townships and small cemeteries. The visual stimuli are sensational and the climate has changed. The harsh Castilian plain has given way to the freshness of the woods. Furthermore,

The Cruz de Fierro, standing at a height of 1,500 m, marks the 'roof' of the Way
(→ STAGE 22, page 126)

The culmination of the journey: the Baroque cathedral of Santiago de Compostela
(→ STAGE 30, page 161)

there are still architectural wonders ahead, such as the monastery of Samos and the towns of Portomarín and Sarria. Lastly, there is Santiago de Compostela itself with its cathedral, which the traveller will contemplate in ecstasy upon the accomplishment of the pilgrimage. The hardiest will, however, carry on for four more days until reaching Cape Finisterre, the legendary end of the world for the Romans.

History of the Way

The origins of Santiago de Compostela and of the ensuing pilgrimage are to be found, as so often in Christian hagiography, in a supernatural occurrence. Early in the ninth century a mysterious glow appeared on mount Libradón, which lies within the limits of the town of Padrón in the interior of Galicia. Some shepherds, seeing that the light came out from among the very rocks, informed the church authorities.

The bishop of the diocese of Iria Flavia, close to Padrón, promptly visited the spot and there found a sarcophagus with the remains of three human beings. It was concluded that the marble coffin could be nothing less than the resting place of Saint James the apostle and two of his most loyal disciples, Atanasio and Teodoro.

King Alfonso II el Casto (the Chaste) was informed and ordered that a sepulchre and a small church be constructed at the place of the find.

And how was it that the remains of the apostle came to be on the Iberian Peninsula? Eight hundred years earlier Saint James, who some historians believe was directly related to Jesus of Nazareth, had witnessed the death of the Son of God and had then left for the Roman province of Hispania to preach His

The statue of Saint James in pilgrim's garb on the dome of Santiago de Compostela cathedral

teachings. It was a short stay and took place somewhere between the years AD 34 and 41. In the year 42 Saint James died in Jerusalem, decapitated by the authorities.

At that time it was a common practice for an apostle to be buried where he had preached

Alfonso II el Casto, the king who laid the foundations for the Way of Saint James at the beginning of the ninth century

Left: the castle of Clavijo, where the famous battle took place. Below: *Victory of the Apostle Saint James on the Moors*, a painting by Juan Carreño.

and it was in connection with this that a miracle occurred. Legend has it that a marble sarcophagus floated the length of the Mediterranean, crossed the Strait of Gibraltar, progressed northward through part of the Atlantic and ran ashore on the Galician coast. It was escorted by the two disciples mentioned above, who would certainly have been the ones who then conveyed it inland.

A miraculous warrior

Eight centuries later, the holy light emanating from the coffin led to its discovery and left no doubt as to the identity of its occupants. Within the political context of the period, this circumstance arose at a time when the Christian kingdoms were under tremendous pressure, resisting as best they could in the north of the peninsula the unstoppable drive of the Muslim armies, who seemed well on their way to conquering the entire territory.

Following repeated defeats and a progressive loss of territory, the morale of the Christians was understandably low. It had become evident that their nobles were being beaten by the enemy on the field of battle and the miracle thus occurred precisely when they most needed a supernatural, invincible leader.

It was then that the turning point came. In 844 the battle of Clavijo took place, so called because it happened beside the hill of that name, on which there was a small military camp, to the south of where the city of Logroño now stands.

On an unequal footing, the Christians prepared to resist the Muslim demand for the yearly tribute of a hundred maidens. Swords were crossed and the Christians quickly realized, in desperation, how out-numbered they were. At that point Saint James, mounted on a white horse, made his appearance, rode determinedly into the fray and turned the tide in the Christians' favour. The day was won and the long road towards the reconquest of the peninsula had begun.

King Ramiro I of Asturias swore that the victory had been won thanks to the interven-tion of the apostle, who from then on was portrayed in a new role, that of *Santiago Matamoros* (Saint James the Moor-slayer). It is as such that he appears in many murals and sculptures, although this portrayal is currently regarded, by many, as politically incorrect.

To show his gratitude for the assistance, the king ordered that pilgrimage should be made to the shrine of the saint. Over the four centuries which followed the route to that destination became a virtual European highway for the passage of people, goods, languages and cultures. Many historians are of the opinion that it was on the strength of the Way of Saint James that Europe as such began to take shape.

From all ends of the continent the faith-ful set out on that pilgrimage, walk-ing for months in order finally to kneel before the apostle's shrine. Thus, the more fre-quently travelled routes became well worn and even today, over a thousand years later, the very same paths continue to be used from different starting points on the European continent to Santiago de Compostela. The one most commonly used by today's pil-grims is the French Way, to which this guide refers, but pilgrims have also followed the *Via Podensis* from Le Puy, the *Via Turonensis* from Char-tres, the *Via de la Plata* (Silver Route), running northward in the west of the Iberian Peninsula, or the *Camino Aragonés* (Aragonese Way) which crosses the Pyrenees at Somport.

Document exhibited at the Santiago de Compostela Pilgrimage Museum

Left: funerary stele at Cirauqui. The classic signs to be found on the French Way (right).

SANTIAGO

IROZ
IROTZ
1 Km.

The monastery of the Virgen Peregrina (Our Lady the Pilgrim) at Sahagún in the province of León. This town took on great importance when, in the Middle Ages, the Cluny order decided to set up one of its headquarters there.

There is also the *Camino de la Costa* (Coastal Way), one of those most used in the Middle Ages, which although very winding had the advantage of being safe from Saracen attack.

The Christian background

Another fundamental event in Christian history, which in turn helped fuel the flow of pilgrims to Santiago de Compostela, occurred towards the end of the ninth century. The Christians lost Jerusalem to the Muslims and were therefore deprived of what was, beside Rome, their most important world pilgrimage destination. As it was thus no longer possible to visit the holy places where Jesus of Nazareth had grown up, preached and suffered martyrdom, many eyes turned towards Santiago de Compostela. It was in part also as a consequence of this circumstance that the shrine grew, over the years, from a modest chapel to a large church and, subsequently, to a great cathedral. The most important initial works within

that process were undertaken in the years 874, 997 and 1075, although they continued over decades. The shrine became a cathedral in the sixteenth century, although the spectacular Baroque façade which is so admired today would not be finished until the eighteenth century.

By the second millennium Santiago de Compostela had become as important as Rome to the Christian pilgrim. The region was living a golden age and the more important monastic orders, such as Cluny or the Knights

The Templar castle at Ponferrada, one of the highlights of the Way

Templar, erected strongholds along the Way, in the form of monasteries or castles. Today you can still visit the most important of these at Sahagún and Ponferrada. At the same time, the Way brought prosperity to the towns which had the good fortune to be crossed by the many travellers. There, churches were built and inns and taverns were opened. In addition, hospices (in the old sense of a place of shelter for travellers) sprang up, to the extent that there came to be dozens of them along the principal pilgrim paths. Furthermore, new townships came into being. These are still readily recognizable by their names: Boadilla del Camino, Espinosa del Camino, Fresno del Camino, Rabanal del Camino, Redecilla del Camino, San Martín del Camino, San Miguel del Camino, San Nicolás del Real Camino and La Virgen del Camino. Nor did those communities necessarily remain modest. Some, like Santo Domingo de la Calzada or Puente la Reina (Gares), came to be of significant size and importance.

The Baroque façade of Santiago de Compostela cathedral in the plaza del Obradoiro

In 1179 Pope Alexander III gave yet greater importance to the pilgrimage by decreeing that a plenary indulgence would be gained by all those who travelled the Way in years when Saint James's Day (25 July) fell on a Sunday. We currently refer to these as Jacobean, Jubilee or Holy Years. In them the number of visitors to Santiago de

The magnificent Roman doorway of the church of Santiago (Saint James) at Puente la Reina (Gares). The town thrived given that it stood at a meeting point of the French Way and the Aragonese Way.

The *crucero* (wayside cross) of Lameiros with a Virgin Mother at the top and a representation of skulls at the base.
On the right, the monument to the pilgrim at Cape Finisterre.

Compostela, great though it already is, can practically triple.

As a consequence of these measures it became all the more frequent for the pilgrimage to be undertaken not just by the common people but also by the monarchs and aristocrats of the time. While they naturally sought to ensure themselves a certain degree of comfort, they still had to endure the hardship of many long days of travelling. By the twelfth century the counts of Barcelona had set up a system to enable their most prominent guests to make the pilgrimage suitably escorted. Even the Catholic Monarchs, King Ferdinand II of Aragon and Queen Isabella I of Castile, undertook the journey in the year 1488, although by then the Way was very much in decline.

Fuelled by the flow of travellers, the towns located on the principal paths grew large and prosperous, becoming important centres of trade. However, the interminable wars that shook Europe from the sixteenth century (above all the Hundred Years War), the spread of the plague and the disappearance of the relics of the apostle, which were missing from 1588 to 1879, caused the Way to fall largely into disuse.

Rebirth

When the cathedral was being remodelled in 1879 some bones appeared. Pope Leo XIII declared that they were the relics of the saint and, little by little, the pilgrimage gained a new lease of life. But it was only towards the end of the last century that a genuine rebirth was witnessed. Various factors entered into play, but two had a decisive impact: in 1987 the Way was declared the first European cultural itinerary; subsequently, in 1993, UNESCO entered it on the World Heritage list. In addition, the journeys that Pope John Paul II made to Santiago de Compostela from 1982 encouraged Catholics to follow his example. At present the Way of Saint James is, as a result, a cultural journey in a continuous state of growth. The next Jacobean year is 2021. With a full decade ahead, all those involved in the conservation and improvement of the Way have time enough to consider how best to maintain the high current level of interest without impairing the unique essence of the pilgrimage.

From Saint-Jean-Pied-de-Port to Roncesvalles
Crossing the Pyrenees
21.2 km • 6 h

Saint-Jean-Pied-de-Port – Honto
1 h 15 min

You leave the charming town of Saint-Jean-Pied-de-Port (Donibane Garazi) by way of the central rue d'Espagne, pass below the clock tower, cross the bridge over the river Nive (Errobi) and go through the Porte d'Espagne. You then at once see large signs indicating the path, which leads upward by way of rue Marechal Harispe.

The gradient is steep and the route is marked by unobtrusive blue tiles. Some of these have been erased by the passage of time, but the path is not difficult to follow. Nearby houses give us a glimpse of the elegant suburbs of the capital of Lower Navarre. There will be practically no rest until you reach Ferme Ithurburia, a combined guesthouse and privately run hostel.

Honto – Auberge Orisson
2 h

The village of Honto lies in the bend

The walls of Saint-Jean-Pied-de-Port

below you as you pass by Ferme Ithurburia. There is an enormous chestnut with a sign below it. The path is still tarmac, but barely 350 m farther on you come to a well-marked, grassy track leading off to the left. This gives you a respite from the road and, although the climb is stiff, allows you to advance in a virtually straight line and avoid a long, roundabout ascent.

Coming out once again onto the road, you will see a fountain with a tap and, 30 m farther up, an orientation table. On this you can locate the peaks of Iparla and the different towns round about. Saint-Jean-Pied-de-Port, where the journey commenced, stands out.

Having paused to enjoy these

Giant chestnut near Honto

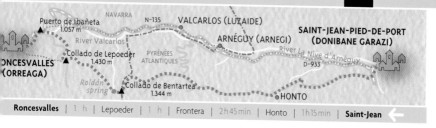

views, you only have to walk up the road for another 15 minutes to reach Auberge Orisson. In the high season this has picnic tables by the door and a shady terrace over the bank, ideal for taking a rest and consulting the map. You have covered over a third of the day's stage and the best parts are yet to come.

Auberge Orisson – Arnéguy turn-off
3 h 15 min

Once again follow the road upward. You are now walking between grassy hillocks. From time to time you will be able to take short cuts which allow you to tread softer terrain and progress in a straighter line. Some of these are marked, while others are so obvious that they need no sign at all. All you have to do is continue to climb while keeping an eye on the black ribbon of the road. After three and a quarter hours, on the right, you will see the turn-off to Arnéguy (an alternative route in winter, see table on page 28). Don't take it; instead follow the sign indicating 'liaison Urkulu'.

Arnéguy turn-off – Fontaine de Roland
4 h

The time has come to part company with the road. While this leads on towards mount Urkulu,

you need to follow a large wooden sign pointing in the direction of Roncesvalles. Barely twenty metres farther on there is a concrete cross inside a fence. The path continues straight on, through soft fields of upland grass, towards the col de Bentartea.

Auberge Orisson

You now come to a narrow stretch between rocks. There you'll find a metal plaque fixed in the stone bearing a long legend in French and, on the right, under the lee of the ridge, the Santiago shelter, which is for use in the event of a storm or difficulty.

You'll begin to see large, leafy beeches, while a wire fence protects you on the right from the danger of a steep slope falling away to the river

Arnéguy below. It is at this point that the gradient which has cost so great an effort for practically four hours becomes less severe. There is little more climbing to do up to the col de Lepoeder. The path, now flatter, is of compact clay. While it can therefore make the going heavy in rainy weather, when dry it provides an agreeable and even soft surface, which is welcome after so many kilometres of tarmac.

The Fontaine de Roland, with its stone bench, is a pleasant spot to have lunch, refill the water bottles and take a rest before undertaking the least difficult part of the stage.

Fontaine de Roland – Col de Lepoeder

5 h

Continue along the same mountain track among ever older and taller beeches and very soon you come to marker stone 199, which stands on the border between France and Spain. There is also a large sign with a map showing your precise position, together with another marker stone indicating the point of entry into the *Comunidad Foral de Navarra* (Chartered Community of

The stage in winter

Pilgrims undertaking this first stage in the low season may encounter a lot of snow between the months of December and May. It is therefore always important to ask at the inns in Saint-Jean-Pied-de-Port whether the Route de Napoleon or, more simply, the *camino de la montaña* (mountain route) is passable. If it is not, the winter route, which is likewise marked perfectly well marked, should be used. This leaves the town via the Porte de France and then follows, in part, the road to Luzaide (Valcarlos). Whenever possible it runs through the woodland and it has some very pleasant stretches by Ganekoleta and Gorozgarai. It is longer but safer. It joins the main route at Ibañeta.

Navarre). Following a few short, fairly undemanding climbs, you reach the 'roof' of the stage, the col de Lepoeder at a height of 1,430 m. To get there follow the yellow arrows painted on the rather big blue signs. The designer may have intended to avoid any possible confusion or wanted to make sure that they would never be obscured by snow and that's why they are so big. Whatever the reason they do seem excessively large.

Pastureland near Lepoeder

Col de Lepoeder – Puerto de Ibañeta

5 h 40 min

Descend towards a hollow where you will find a post with various signs. From here you can take either the direct route through the wood down to Roncesvalles (Orreaga), which is rather steep, or the easier path to Ibañeta. The signs recommend the second, as do we, albeit only so as not to miss the historic point where the earlier pilgrims rejoiced in having overcome the formidable Pyrenees and, according to legend, the death of Roland, which gave rise to the epic poem *Chanson de Roland*, took place.

The descent follows the GR-11, is well marked and cuts out the bends of the road. In little more than half an hour you reach Ibañeta, where you can take a certain pride in having now overcome the north face of the mountain range. The day's walk will soon be over.

Orientation table and villages of Lower Navarre in the background

Puerto de Ibañeta – Roncesvalles (Orreaga)

6 h

A straightforward descent by the side of the road leads in less than half an hour to the collegiate church of Roncesvalles. The hostel does not open until 16.00. You can visit the church, the chapter house and the museum. In addition, less than 50 m farther down the road, there is a hermitage and the crypt where Roland is said to have died. In the evening there is a mass at which the pilgrims receive a blessing. The first stage of the journey is the toughest, precisely because it is the first and entails, furthermore, a climb of 1,200 m, but now it is over.

Eating

The best plan is to carry a light packed lunch. Food is available only at Auberge Orisson, which is too close to the start of the stage. In Roncesvalles there are no shops, but dinner can be had at its two restaurants.

Sleeping

A broad range of accommodation is available in Saint-Jean-Pied-de-Port, but the municipal hostel is currently closed. There is, among others, Auberge Ultreia at rue de la Citadelle 8 (telephone 0033 680 884 622), open from April to October.

The hostel at Roncesvalles (telephone 0034 948 760 000) is open all year. It provides basic services only.

For fuller information on all hostels on this and all the following stages, see the list at the end of this guide.

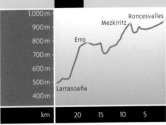

1.000 m
900 m
800 m
700 m
600 m
500 m
400 m

Roncesvalles
Mezkiritz
Erro
Larrasoaña

km   20   15   10   5

From Roncesvalles to Larrasoaña
Pyrenean beech woods

23.5 km • 6 h 35 min

Roncesvalles – Burguete (Auritz)
45 min

On taking the road downward out of Roncesvalles you immediately come upon a large sign reading 'to Santiago, 790 km'. This might prove a little discouraging, although you may find some consolation in the knowledge that 790 km is the distance by road, whereas the pathways provide numerous short cuts. And look on the bright side: a great journey full of sensations lies ahead.

Not many metres farther on, another sign invites you to follow the path through a leafy beech wood on a carpet of leaves. It is wise to tread carefully. The path is in shadow and there may still be puddles on the ground even weeks after the last rains. Little holly trees adorn the path, which leads just slightly downward. Thirty minutes after starting out you reach the white cross of Roland.

At this point you leave the wood

The collegiate church of Roncesvalles

and take the road. You are now on the outskirts of Burguete (Auritz), a typical town of the Navarre side of the Pyrenees where big houses, their fronts white with the stone partially showing, line the road. As you walk down the main street you will see the family crests which many of them display.

Burguete (Auritz) – Espinal (Autizberri)
1 h 45 min

The office of Banco Santander marks the point where you should turn, go downhill and cross the wooden bridge over the river Urrobi. Then walk for a good while on a level, broad, unsurfaced track, observed by the many birds perched on the fences to the side. Pass a dairy farm and go over various stone bridges; some streams are forded simply by means of stepping stones. The path

Sunrise at Burguete

ZUBIRI
River Arga
N-135
Alto de Erro
801 m
LINTZOAIN
BISCARRETA
N-135
River Erro
Alto de Mezkiritz
922 m
ESPINAL
(AURIZBERRI)
River Urrobi
RONCESVALLES
(ORREAGA)
N-135
BURGUETE
(AURITZ)
RASOAÑA

| Larrasoaña | 1h | Zubiri | 3h 50 min | Espinal | 1h | Burguete | 45 min | **Roncesvalles** |

Bridge over the river Urrobi

is clearly indicated with markers and the traditional scallop shell symbols. You join the road a quarter of an hour before reaching Espinal (Autizberri), where the street leading into the town takes you past an enormous *pelota* court.

Espinal (Autizberri) – Alto de Mezkiritz
2 h 15 min

Moving on towards Alto de Mezkiritz, take a muddy pathway which becomes progressively narrower. It leads upward between wire fences intended to keep in the livestock. Provided you follow the markers, there is no chance of getting lost. You will come to a road, cross it and there see a stele which, in Basque, Spanish and French, invites the traveller to say a Hail Mary. Behind it are the signs showing where the Way

continues. The path now leads downward but the going remains heavy. After about a kilometre, however, the mud gives way to a cement surface patterned to imitate paving stones. The going at once becomes easier but take care not to slip, particularly in the early hours when there may be ice. This leads into the farming village of Biscarreta.

Alto de Mezkiritz – Biscarreta
3 h

Cross this village by way of the main street. Towards the end you pass a shop where you can buy food and directly opposite there is a drinking fountain. Upon leaving the village you once again encounter the imitation paving-stone path which ends at a fork where it is easy to take a wrong turn. Don't follow the signs indicating 'robledal de Muskilda' but instead take the other path to the right. Otherwise the way is well marked.

Biscarreta – Lintzoain
3 h 15 min

It takes just a quarter of an hour to reach Lintzoain. The town is small but the houses are imposing. A number of their owners now combine their traditional farming activities with the rural tourism trade. It is time to take a short rest and prepare yourself for the climb to Alto de Erro.

Lintzoain – Alto de Erro
4 h 30 min

From Lintzoain you take a very good, correctly marked, broad

Pilgrims' fountain at Biscarreta

track. Stony at first, it subsequently becomes soft and may be muddy. Scented pines and decorative box trees border the way and provide shade. The path leads steadily upward and is steep at times. You come out onto the road and cross it.

Alto de Erro – Zubiri
5 h 25 min

Descend through a leafy wood, a geographic feature that you will see very little of again for three weeks. Pass by the old Venta de Agorreta, formerly a pilgrims' hostel. There are some signs which have a rather home-made look but still serve their purpose well.

Carry on downward along an undemanding path until you reach the valley floor. You soon come to the outskirts of Zubiri, which many pilgrims make the end of the stage, given that it is worth visiting and has good facilities. However, as it has not been a long day, it is better to keep going. This makes the next stage, the third, shorter and you'll have time to look round Pamplona.

Abandoned boots

The two Pyrenean stages are hard, and they come at the very beginning. It is therefore necessary to be prepared, both mentally and physically, and above all to review, before starting off, the equipment you are going to use. It is by no means unusual to see broken-down boots abandoned along the Way. Those shown in the photograph, taken at Alto de Erro, must have given up the ghost in the woods of Navarre.

Zubiri – Ilarratz
6 h

To take a look at Zubiri you must cross its medieval bridge, known as the *puente de la Rabia* (the Rabies bridge). It is said that the inhabitants of the town used to make their domestic animals walk around its central pillar, as it was believed that they would thus be kept safe from that feared disease. The town is pretty and worth a visit, but the noise from its magnesite processing factory is rather more than background and detracts from the rural charm.

Barely a kilometre farther along the Way, which is well marked in this stretch, you come to Ilarratz, a pleasant village with a fountain where you can afford a last break before taking on the final section of the day's walk. From here you travel through wooded country. The path is not very wide, but is good enough to allow a smooth progression, leaving the factory noise behind. You pass by another group of houses at the hamlet of Ezkirotz. The path runs close by the river Arga and from time to time offers splendid views.

Ilarratz – Larrasoaña
6 h 35 min

According to historical records, Larrasoaña has been giving shelter to pilgrims for almost a thousand years, although these days most travellers choose to spend the night at Zubiri. In the town centre you will find the municipal hostel

Bridge over the river Arga at Larrasoaña

and the thirteenth-century church of San Nicolás de Bari (Saint Nicholas). The town is no longer a pilgrims' paradise, but by extending the day's stage you will have the advantage, tomorrow, of reaching Pamplona, the capital of Navarre, at a relatively early hour. You also avoid the unpleasant noise of the factory at Zubiri.

Eating
Larrasoaña is not a place for dining out. There is a bar, but it does not keep regular opening hours and may be closed in the low season. The best plan is to buy what you need at Zubiri or at one of the towns you pass through. At Biscarreta there is a shop selling bread and fresh fruit. Most of the others focus on canned food. The Larrasoaña hostel itself sells a limited selection of food, but if you opt for this you will have to make do with what may be available.

Sleeping
The municipal hostel (telephone 0034 605 505 489) is open all day, but the *hospitalera* does not come until three in the afternoon. Anyone arriving before that time may settle in, if the door is open, and subsequently make arrangements with her for the stay. There are also three boarding houses in the town, but they are generally closed in the low season. They open from May.

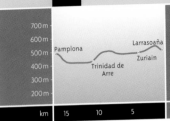

From Larrasoaña to Pamplona (Iruña)
A walk beside the river Arga

700m
600m
500m — Pamplona   Larrasoaña
400m   Zuriain
300m   Trinidad de
200m   Arre

km   15   10   5

12.8 km • 3 h 35 min

Larrasoaña – Akerreta
10 min

You may well wish to begin by taking a look back at the Pyrenean mountain ranges you crossed on the first two stages of the Way. Not until you reach the Montes de Oca, in about a week, will you see mountains of any size again, although they are by no means comparable in height and extent.

You leave Larrasoaña via a cement track which leads slightly upward, thus avoiding the main road, where vehicles pass close by at dangerous speeds. There is barely time to warm up before you reach the village of Akerreta,

which has a guesthouse, a church and little else. This is farming country and you will have to pass through occasional wooden gates bearing signs in Basque reminding us to leave them closed. From time to time some *pottoka* (Basque ponies) may come up to sniff in curiosity at the traveller's backpack.

Akerreta – Zuriain
1 h

The path follows a level course though a wood. On your right the river Arga guides you as reliably as Ariadne's thread. Just before you reach Zuriain there is a fountain down by the water's edge, reached by means of steps with a wooden handrail. In Zuriain you will encounter something which will soon become ubiquitous: the drinks vending machine. This phenomenon has become fairly commonplace all along the Way from here, but in this part of Navarre it is omnipresent.

Zuriain – Irotz
1 h 25 min

A short, easy walk takes you to Irotz. From Zuriain there is the alternative of taking a riverside path, likewise leading to Pamplona, frequented by cyclists

Medieval bridge over the river Arga

A pilgrim passing through a gate near Akerreta. On the left, an old plaque at Trinidad de Arre.

and people out for a stroll. Our route, however, follows the official Way of Saint James, which is, furthermore, three kilometres shorter, although the final stretch runs through a series of urban avenues distinguishable only in that from time to time you see signs indicating that you are leaving one municipality and entering another.

Irotz – Zabaldika
1 h 50 min

On our last visit, in the spring of 2009, the path out of Irotz was cut off and a disconcerting sign gave travellers the stern warning that power lines had fallen. It was therefore necessary to detour via the cement riverside walk for half an hour until reaching a picnic area known as Zabaldika. This is

a good place for a short rest, given that although the day's walk will not be a long one and you have already covered almost two thirds, you face a climb up a stony path. At Zabaldika there are public toilets, picnic tables and stone barbecues.

Rejoin the path, following the plainly visible yellow arrows, in the direction of Arleta, an enormous country house whose very stones speak of its splendid past. It even has a hermitage attached for use as a private chapel. When passing by the house, the path levels off for a moment. From here you have the best views of the valley of the Arga. The river has accompanied you nearly all day, but you will now lose sight of it until reaching Pamplona.

You enter the town by way of the calle Mayor (high street), a pedestrian precinct with bars on both sides offering an enticing array of tapas. Soon, however, you come out onto a long straight avenue which leads you direct to Burlada.

Trinidad de Arre – Burlada
2 h 55 min

While this is only a short stretch, it feels strange, after the solitary pastures of the Pyrenees and the idyllic rural villages of Navarre, to be walking along a pavement, even though it is, admittedly, broad, smooth and well marked with the customary yellow arrows. Certain striking buildings, such as the school of agriculture at Villava, are worth attention, but the natural habitat of the pilgrim is rural rather than urban. This is a feeling that you may experience again when entering other towns and cities along the Way. It is likely to be particularly strong in Pamplona (Iruña), a very dynamic city whose old quarter is always teeming with life.

School of agriculture at Villava

Zabaldika – Trinidad de Arre
2 h 35 min

Descend somewhat abruptly by a stony path, take an underpass to cross the highway and, just 45 minutes after leaving Zabaldika, you find yourself on the medieval bridge of Trinidad de Arre with its six arches. It is worth pausing in the middle to look down at the gentle waters of the river Ultzama. The medieval hostel used to stand just at the other end.

Dates to be avoided

Of the four cities which the French Way crosses, Pamplona offers the fewest facilities for pilgrims. The hostels open only in the season (from Holy Week to October). Outside that period one has to go to a hotel. Travellers should take note that the week of San Fermín (from 6 July) and carnival are to be avoided at all costs: the city is full, prices rise and sleep is impossible.

Burlada – Pamplona
3 h 35 min

Following that urban section, you come once again to the river Arga, which you last saw mid-morning. Here your path crosses the riverside walk which you could have taken at Irotz. Before you is the Magdalena bridge, a highlight of the pilgrimage, marked with a cross and commemorative plaques.

On crossing the bridge you at once come to the walls of the city of Pamplona. From this point you must pay closer attention to the signs marking the Way, because they are at times positioned so unobtrusively that they can be missed. Turn to the right, go alongside the city wall for a couple of minutes and you will find yourself between two high walls which lead up to the archway marking the entrance to calle del Carmen. Just to its right stands the inn known in the city as the 'albergue de los alemanes' (the German hostel).

The urban part of the route concludes, symbolically, at the door of the cathedral. Just as the Way always passes by the main church in the smaller towns, so in the cities it runs to the cathedral. Subsequently, the exit is via the central streets of Mercaderes, Mayor and Bosquecillo, towards the citadel.

Today's stage was made shorter in order to allow enough time to take a look around the city. An interesting visit lies in store (see pages 38 to 41).

The Los Fueros monument in Pamplona

Eating

On this stage it is not possible to buy provisions before reaching Trinidad de Arre. Some pilgrims will, at all events, find no difficulty in waiting until they reach Pamplona, where there is a vast range of restaurants. Some of those in the old quarter are very well known, but be warned that their prices tend to be very high. Menus specifically for pilgrims are not, in general, to be found, but what's on offer is so varied that everyone can usually find something suited to his or her budget and needs.

Sleeping

There are two hostels in Pamplona. The albergue de Jesús y María (telephone 0034 948 222 644) is the municipal hostel and is run by the Asociación de Amigos del Camino. It is in calle Compañía, by the cathedral and is open all year except for the week of San Fermín and Christmas. The other is Casa Paderborn (telephone 0034 948 211 712) in calle Playa de Caparroso, reached shortly after crossing the Magdalena bridge. Run by a German association, it is popularly known as the German hostel. It opens from March to October.

Pamplona (Iruña)
The city of the running of the bulls

Distance
behind you
57.5 km

The cathedral

The current Gothic cathedral was built between the fourteenth and fifteenth centuries. It is only from the inside that the beauty of this style may be appreciated, as the main façade, with its twin towers, is in a more sober, neoclassical vein.

In the central nave you find the sepulchre of Charles III

and Leonor of Navarre, whose recumbent figures are accompanied by an impressive body of mourners. It is to be borne in mind that the monarchs used to be crowned here and that it was even, at one time, the seat of government, where the parliament of Navarre convened. The cathedral stands on a promontory which archaeologists have identified as the site of the ancient Roman city.

The point where the riverside walk and the traditional path converge

The citadel

This fort was erected on orders given by King Philip II in 1571. It has the classic star shape, which, in theory, made it unassailable. It fulfilled its role as stronghold of the city more or less effectively into well into the twentieth century, when it was converted into a park for the use and enjoyment

The city hall (left) and, above, the monument to the running of the bulls.

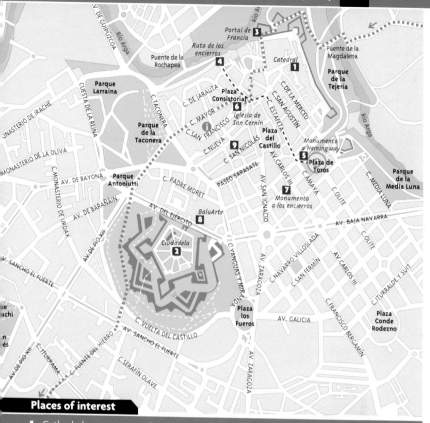

Places of interest

1 Cathedral
2 Citadel
3 Portal de Francia
4 Bull-running route
5 Monument to Hemingway
6 Church of San Cernín
7 Monument to the running of the bulls
8 BaluArte
9 Calle San Nicolás

Eating

Bars and restaurants abound in Pamplona, particularly in the old quarter, and there is consequently no danger of going hungry provided, of course, that one has a little money. Be warned that in the 'bares de poteo' (tapas bars) the bill can go up rapidly and the type of food may not be the most appropriate for a person who needs to keep in good physical shape. In this area of the city the pilgrim may, in contrast, have some difficulty finding shops where they can buy provisions. It is better to try in the new part of the city, to the south of the bullring.

Sleeping

The first hostel that the pilgrim comes to, just after crossing the Magdalena bridge and entering the city, is Casa Paderborn (telephone 0034 948 211 712), known as the German hostel, at calle Playa de Caparroso, 6. It opens from March to October. The municipal hostel, albergue de Jesús y María (telephone 0034 948 222 644), is in calle Compañía, by the cathedral. It is open all year except for the week of San Fermín and Christmas. There is, in addition, a vast range of hotels and boarding houses.

The week of San Fermín, when prices can quintuple, and carnival are best avoided, as the city is crowded and the noise goes on all night.

of the citizens. Today it is one of the city's most popular green areas where, in addition, you may see works of art and shows are regularly organized. The pilgrims' path crosses this park via the Vuelta del Castillo (the citadel's glacis), goes past the San Nicolás gateway and heads north out of the city.

The pilgrim enters and leaves Pamplona by way of medieval bridges

Portal de Francia

On arriving at the city of Pamplona pilgrims must cross the river Arga and then head for the maze of streets which make up the old quarter. To that effect they must climb the steps that lead to the impressive gateway in the walls known as the Portal de Francia, a great arch bearing an imposing coat of arms. Its official name is Portal de Zumalacárregui, but citizens and visitors alike appear to disregard this.

The bull-running route

During the second week of July hundreds of people take their lives in their hands by running, in front of a group of bulls, through a series of old-quarter streets leading to the bullring. Some of those streets, such as the legendary calle Estafeta or cuesta de Santo Domingo, may already be familiar to you, if only by name, given the media coverage they receive during the *fiesta*. Throughout the rest of the year tourists may, at a more leisurely pace, find visitor information relating to the event on the panels placed along the route.

Getting the stamp in Pamplona

Although a large city, the first of those through which the Way passes, Pamplona is not a particularly easy place for the pilgrim. One of the two hostels is closed from October to March. This can complicate the task of getting the necessary stamp on the pilgrim's pass. In theory you can go to any church, but most of them are open only at the times of service, when the priest is busy. The simplest solution is to go to the tourist information office in plaza San Francisco (calle Hilarión Eslava).

The monument to Hemingway

The American writer Ernest Hemingway was a regular visitor to Pamplona. As he was attracted by the bullfights and the running of the bulls, the location of this hyper-realist bust, just at the point where the animals enter the ring, seems only appropriate.

The church of San Cernín (Saint Saturnin)

Few people outside Pamplona know that the patron saint of the city is not Fermin but Saturnin, the first evangelist of Pamplona. His church is in calle San Saturnino. Although originally Romanesque in style, following extensive remodelling it now has a Gothic appearance.

Monument to the running of the bulls

This vividly captures one of those tense moments where the runners are so dangerously close to the horns. It is very realistic, lacking nothing other than the shouts and the smell of sweat.

BaluArte

Patxi Mangado is the architect who designed this spectacular conference centre which, in addition, hosts the city's main artistic events. A visit is well worthwhile not only to admire the building but also to consult the programme, as there are always theatrical and dance performances, exhibitions and other cultural events of potential interest to the visitor.

The plaza del Castillo, centre of the city's social life, and (below) the interior of the Café Iruña.

Calle San Nicolás

When walking around the old quarter, visitors will repeatedly find themselves in calle San Nicolás. This is where *poteo*, the social custom of doing the round of tapas bars, is most practised. There is a profusion of bars and restaurants and the citizens traditionally come out in their best clothes to take a walk there in the evening. The pilgrim's visit should always take in the fortress church of San Nicolás (Saint Nicholas). It stands in a wider section of the street and its tall tower dominates the old part of the city.

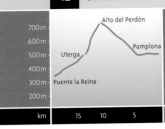

Alto del Perdón

700m
600m
500m   Uterga
400m
300m   Puente la Reina
200m

km   15   10   5

From Pamplona (Iruña) to Puente la Reina (Gares)
Where main pilgrimage paths meet

20.1 km • 5 h 35 min

Pamplona – Cizur Menor
1 h 5 min

The route out of Pamplona is pleasant, barely touching industrial areas or the kind of suburbs where the pilgrim feels out of place.

The route is marked, but while still inside the city you may miss the signs if you're not careful. However, it is quite straightforward: set off from the cathedral though the streets Carmen, Mayor and Bosquecillo, go past the gateway of San Nicolás and across the citadel park by way of a surfaced walk known as the Vuelta del Castillo. On leaving the park cross avenida de Sancho el Fuerte and take calle Fuente del Hierro in the direction of the university. Then go down past the gardens of the faculties until you come to the medieval bridge over the river Sadar. You should reach it some 40 minutes after having started out.

Plaza del Castillo, Pamplona

Once on the other side of the river you are in the outskirts of Pamplona. Here you take a *bidegorri* ('red path' in Basque). These are tracks which have been surfaced for use by cyclists and are coloured red. The pedestrian one, which has a somewhat damaged surface, leads slightly uphill and takes you to a bridge in the form of a cage spanning the railway line and one of the city's main ring roads. After crossing the bridge you at once come to the town of Cizur Menor.

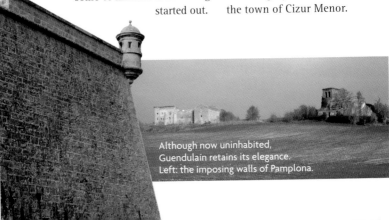

Although now uninhabited, Guendulaín retains its elegance.
Left: the imposing walls of Pamplona.

Cizur Menor –Zariquiegui
2 h 30 min

Cizur Menor is on the way to becoming the favoured end for the previous stage, as many pilgrims prefer the great hospitality and untroubled rest provided by its hostel in calle Belzeta (open all year) to the noise and discomfort sometimes encountered in Pamplona. The disadvantage, however, is that if you make Cizur Menor your stage destination you severely limit your opportunities to do a little urban tourism. You must decide which you prefer.

Leaving Cizur Menor behind, take a broad, level, unsurfaced track running between cornfields. After half an hour the track begins to narrow and is soon no more than a path. It is, however, very well marked. For a time it ascends, almost imperceptibly but constantly, until you draw near to Zariquiegui, at which point it becomes a slope. This is the preamble to the difficult part of this stage, the Alto del Perdón. Zariquiegui has no facilities for pilgrims, but if the church of San Miguel (Saint Michael) is open don't miss the opportunity to enter and admire the altar with its reredos and the Gothic style which characterizes the church as a whole.

Reredos of the church of Zariquiegui

Zariquiegui – Alto del Perdón
3 h 5 min

The night before, at the hostel, you may have heard others talk about the fearsome Alto del Perdón. That is, however, talk and nothing more. The climb is undemanding, although the path is stony, and takes little more than half an hour. Furthermore, you are sheltered from the wind by the side of the mountain to your left. A few minutes after leaving Zariquiegui you will come to the fountain called *fuente de la Teja*, where, according to legend, the traveller could formerly obtain water at the price of selling his soul to the devil. Perhaps too many agreed to that deal, as nowadays the fountain is dry for most of the year.

Figure on the Alto del Perdón

Alto del Perdón – Uterga
3 h 55 min

When you get your first view of the Alto del Perdón from the path you can immediately appreciate why it was chosen as the site for a wind farm. A strong wind blows constantly, leaving the landscape clean and allowing you a view of both plains to the north and south of the crest. At the highest point there is a cross, together with a sculpture, erected by the electricity company, consisting of a group of figures cut from sheet metal with an inscription reading 'where the way of the wind crosses that of the

Ancestral house in Óbanos

stars'. Cross the road and follow the arrows, which at this point mingle with those of a GR footpath, and commence a rather steep descent made slippery in places by the pebbles lying on the clay soil. Luckily the tall box trees and a little holm oak wood will shelter you from the wind.

On the way down you will find, from time to time, steps consisting simply of wooden sleepers. These make the descent easier and provide a respite for your knees. There are also some benches where you can sit and take a rest. At the bottom of the slope lies Uterga.

Uterga – Muruzábal
4 h 40 min

A path, initially stony and uncomfortable but subsequently sandy and pleasant, leads out of Uterga between fields and fruit trees. In spring, particularly, the cherry trees are a delight. It takes little more than half an hour to reach Muruzábal, a village from which you can make the detour to Eunate (see box). Normally you can expect to arrive in Muruzábal a little after midday. You

---

Detour to Eunate

Upon entering Muruzábal you will find a sign on a wall encouraging you to visit the church of Santa María de Eunate (Saint Mary of Eunate). If you are feeling strong enough, the detour is well worthwhile. The return walk (5 km) takes a little over an hour, but you are rewarded with a view of this unusual church surrounded by the ring of arches from which its name is derived (*ehun ate* means 'hundred gates' in Basque). It stands just a little way off the road in a tranquil rustic setting. The church is octagonal and the ring of arches around it likewise has eight faces. This circumstance has fuelled theories that it may have Templar origins. It has also been said that it is modelled after the Dome of the Rock in Jerusalem. The vault in turn has eight ribs, but no central boss.

The majestic bridge over the river Arga at Puente la Reina. On the right, corbels.

can have lunch at the only bar and then ask the owner to look after your backpack while you visit Eunate. However, those who feel stronger may prefer to carry their packs with them to Eunate, bearing in mind that the French Way links up there with the Aragonese Way and it is therefore possible to go on to Puente la Reina, as planned, without having to walk the 2.5 km back to Muruzábal.

Muruzábal – Óbanos
4 h 50 min

An easy walk along a broad, well-marked track brings you in less than 20 minutes to Óbanos. The gateway to the town, the monumental church and cross and some ancestral houses with their coats of arms are the most striking features. You will also note that the symbol of the Way, the scallop shell, is set in metal in the concrete pavement at the points of entry and exit.

Óbanos – Puente la Reina
5 h 35 min

A country road leads from Óbanos to Puente la Reina in barely half an hour. Puente la Reina is one of the most emblematic points of the Way on its passage through Navarre. It is here that it also converges, 'officially', with the route that comes from the Somport pass in Huesca.

Eating
There are bars or restaurants where you can stop for lunch in Cizur Menor, Uterga, Muruzábal and Óbanos. In the first and the last of those towns there are also shops where you can buy provisions, if you prefer to have a picnic. Dinner can be had at one of the various bar/restaurants in Puente la Reina which

have menus for pilgrims at competitive prices. There are also shops where provisions can be purchased for the following day.

Sleeping
There are three hostels in Puente la Reina. The albergue de los Padres Reparadores (telephone 0034 948 340 050) is next to the church of the Crucifijo (the Crucifix) and

is open all year. The Jakue (telephone 0034 948 341 017) is on the main road and opens from March to October. The Santiago Apóstol (telephone 0034 948 340 220) is to be reached by going over the bridge and up a slope. It opens from April to October. There are also two hotels, but it is wise to check whether they are open if you plan to come in the low season.

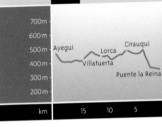

From Puente la Reina (Gares) to Ayegui
Steep inclines and wind

20.4 km • 5 h 45 min

Puente la Reina – Mañeru
1 h 20 min

It is well worth taking a walk around Puente la Reina before leaving it. The town developed thanks to the passage of pilgrims during the Middle Ages, when the Way was at its height. The most noteworthy buildings are in and around calle Mayor, where most of the facilities are similarly centred. After passing by the Padres Reparadores monastery, you come to the church of Santiago (Saint James), with its two Romanesque doors and Gothic nave, then to the church of the Crucifijo (the Crucifix) with its two Gothic naves, a rare feature in Navarre, and next to the church of San Pedro (Saint Peter), which houses the figure of the revered Virgen del Txori. The word *txori* means bird in Basque and the Virgin is so called because, according to legend, a little bird used to come regularly to clean her face.

The town's best-known monument is the beautiful Romanesque bridge,

Monument to the pilgrim at Puente la Reina

with its six arches, over the Arga. It is via this bridge, one of the most impressive you will see along the Way, that you leave the town and every pilgrim feels something special when surmounting its hump back.

After crossing the bridge take a broad track beside the river. The roar of traffic comes from overhead, but the vehicles pass by unseen. There are some signs marking this 'provisional' stretch of the Way, opened up to replace the original route invaded by the road. You will make easy progress on level ground for about an hour, but before reaching Mañeru you come to a long, steep slope with reddish soil and rather a lot of large stones which make the going awkward.

Medieval bridge   Roman road   **PUENTE LA REINA (GARES)**
ESTELLA (LIZARRA)   A-12   Roman road   A-12
EGUI   N-111   LORCA   CIRAUQUI   MAÑERU
River Ega   VILLATUERTA   River Salado   River Arga
A-12

Ayegui | 1h35min | Villatuerta | 55min | Lorca | 1h55min | Mañeru | 1h20min | **Puente la Reina** ←

Mañeru – Cirauqui
1 h 50 min

The pilgrim follows the winding streets of Mañeru, admiring its great, well-restored houses proudly displaying their coats of arms. The route takes you along calle Forzosa, calle Esperanza and plaza de los Fueros, then passes close by the cemetery. From here you can see the outline of the next village. The two are linked by vineyards and a dusty trail. This is a view that epitomises the character of this part of the Way of Saint James.

The old quarter of Cirauqui

Cirauqui – Lorca
3 h 15 min

Cirauqui is another town with architectural delights which, to the majority of visitors, come as a surprise, as the name of the place is not normally to be found on any list of major tourist attractions. The houses are imposing, with massive main walls and façades. You go under arches and along narrow streets towards the upper part of the town. Curiously, the path leads under the very portico of the Town Hall, which has the look of a blind alley. There are two medieval churches in the town, that of San Román (Saint Raymond) and that of Santa Catalina (Saint Catherine), both with magnificent doorways.

As the town stands on a promontory, you leave it by way of a sharp descent and immediately come to the Roman road which linked Bordeaux and Astorga. It is pleasant to look at

Disquieting memorials

From the very outset the traveller encounters, from time to time, simple monuments or plaques dedicated to pilgrims who died of different causes on the Way: pedestrian fatalities, falling off bikes, heat stroke, hypothermia, heart attack ... This serves to remind us that, although the Way may not be difficult, it is necessary to be in good physical shape and to be alert to dangers.

and well preserved. However, what you see are the foundations, which were originally covered with a finer layer of gravel. As a result it is not comfortable for walking and can be dangerous for cyclists, who must watch where they put their wheels and beware of the vibrations. The road leads to a bridge, likewise Roman, which crosses the river Iguste and helpfully avoids the traffic on the Pamplona–Logroño highway.

The Way is well marked and offers interesting views of the avant-garde buildings to the sides which reflect the prosperity of the wineries of Navarre.

The Santo Sepulcro (Holy Sepulchre) church in Estella

Lorca – Villatuerta
4 h 10 min

Lorca's calle Mayor is the virtual backbone of the town. Halfway along it there is a small garden area where you might want to take a rest, bearing in mind that you have now covered more than half the day's journey. The terrain round about gives the pilgrim no comfort. There is no shade and the wind blows dust out of the vineyards. The stage is therefore more tiring than some, although it entails no particular difficulty in terms of length or terrain.

On leaving Lorca notice that the landscape is starting to change, as the vineyards are giving way to cornfields, but this will not last long. More days filled with grapes lie ahead in La Rioja. Although you will be going downhill practically all the way to Villatuerta, the descents are no longer so steep as those you previously encountered.

Villatuerta – Estella (Lizarra)
5 h 25 min

The current Way avoids the centre of Villatuerta, going, instead, through the lower part of the town. However, you will still be able to stock up on provisions, as you will find grocery stores and other shops, together with various bars.

A flight of steps leads downward out of Villatuerta. Just before you cross the road you will see the chilling memorial to a Canadian pilgrim who was run over at this point. Go down to the river, crossing it by means of a wooden bridge built in the form of an unusually pronounced arch, as though in Japanese

Fountain at Villatuerta

style. The rest of the stage, up to Estella, is easy, although a further upward stretch still lies ahead to test your stamina.

Estella – Ayegui
5 h 45 min

The route into Estella could hardly be more spectacular. Just before reaching the built-up area you pass by the Santo Sepulcro (Holy Sepulchre) church, where you should pause to admire the doorway and the blend of Romanesque and Gothic styles. Go along the rúa de los Curtidores, which dates back to the more prosperous era of the Way of Saint James. Once inside the city as such, you come to the church of San Pedro (Saint Peter), which is Romanesque, has arches revealing an oriental influence and a magnificent cloister. Then you find the church of San Miguel (Saint Michael), the monastery of Santo Domingo (Saint Dominic) and the palace of the monarchs of Navarre, just opposite the church of San Pedro (Saint Peter). You need only look at the great armorial crests on the fronts of the buildings in order to appreciate the historic importance of the place.

Detail of a façade in Ayegui

Leave Estella by crossing a bridge, which is barely noticeable, over the river Ega and then walk upward through the suburbs to the adjacent town of Ayegui. The Way is marked with metal representations of scallop shells set in the ground. There is little of note in Ayegui, but the town has the dual advantage of being sufficiently far from Estella to be less affected by the fight for a bed at the hostels at the times when the flow of pilgrims is at its highest, but at the same time close enough to enable it to be used as a base so you can go down to the city for dinner. Between the two towns there stands a sign indicating the distance to Santiago de Compostela: 666 km, the number of the devil.

ALBERGUE

Eating
There are shops for buying provisions in Mañeru, Cirauqui, Lorca, Villatuerta and, logically, Estella. Early in the day bread might be difficult to find in the smaller towns, as it often comes in from bakeries outside. All the towns on the stage have bars and restaurants, although some may be closed, or may open at a later hour, in the low season.

Sleeping
Estella can be overcrowded and for this reason we have suggested ending this stage at Ayegui, where the municipal hostel (telephone 0034 948 554 311) is in the local sports centre. It is modern and very comfortable, although cold in the winter. The hostel and sports centre share showers and baths. Most pilgrims instead choose to end the stage in Estella, just a kilometre away, where there are three hostels: Hospital de Peregrinos (telephone 0034 948 550 200), run by the Asociación de Amigos del Camino, open all year except at Christmas, albergue San Miguel (telephone 0034 948 550 431), likewise open all year, and albergue de Anfas (telephone 0034 680 459 798), open from May to September.

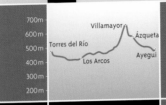

From Ayegui to Torres del Río
Fountains running with wine

23.5 km • 6 h 30 min

Ayegui – Irache
20 min

On leaving the Ayegui sports centre you travel along a road lined with factories and business premises. This upper part of the town looks rather like an industrial estate and is not the loveliest journey for the traveller. Soon, however, the yellow arrows point towards a broad, stony track which takes you away from the industrial district of Ayegui and leads, in little more than a quarter of an hour, to something quite unique, the fountain of Irache. This was installed by a local winery and has two taps, one delivering water and the other wine. There is no charge, but the inscription on the fountain asks the traveller to exercise moderation. Bearing in mind that you will normally pass by this point early in the day and, furthermore, that a web cam is watching, it is advisable not to over-indulge. It is better just to have a taste of the wine and then move on.

Soon afterwards

The fountain of Irache, from which wine flows

we come to the impressive monastery of Irache. These days it is closed and unoccupied, but the size of the building and the church it incorporates on the left side bear witness to its magnificent past. It is apparently to become a *parador* (a state-run luxury hotel), although no opening date has as yet been set.

AZQUETA

Irache – Ázqueta
1 h 25 min

Leaving the fountain and the monastery behind, walk for about half an hour along a surfaced road by a housing development. Go past a camping site and then take a good path, with ascents and descents,

Fuente de los Moros

through a small, cool, oak wood. To the right there is a splendid view of the rocky face of the Sierra de Urbasa. You then come to Ázqueta, where a character by the name of Pablito de las Varas has made himself famous by making presents of sticks to pilgrims. He is not always waiting by the side of the Way, but those eager to obtain the support of a stick will be able to find his house without difficulty, as everyone in the town knows where he lives.

Ázqueta – Villamayor de Monjardín
1 h 55 min

You leave Ázqueta via the valley floor and then begin a climb up a broad, dusty track running between vineyards. This is without doubt the most beautiful section of the stage and typifies the landscape of this part of the Way. The church tower of the next town, Villamayor, can be seen from the very moment you leave Ázqueta. The trail is winding but easy and takes you past a building with a steeply pitched, gable roof. Two large arches give passage to the inside, where there is a cistern of considerable size. This is the Fuente de los Moros (the Fountain of the Moors). It was restored barely

quite recently, but dates back to the Middle Ages. Its origins are unclear, but some documents show that it may have been used for ritual bathing or simply for the performance of ablutions, which pilgrims would no doubt have welcomed when travelling these dusty tracks.

From here again you will see, at a lower level, the church tower of Villamayor de Monjardín. On the rest

A pilgrim with a horse.
On the left, the church of Santa María (Saint Mary) in Los Arcos.

of this stretch the going remains easy, although just before reaching the town you come to a fairly steep descent: be careful not to slip on the sandy soil.

Villamayor de Monjardín – Los Arcos
4 h 35 min

It is worth pausing to take a look around Villamayor de Monjardín. Up on the hill stand the ruins of the old castle of San Esteban (Saint Steven) de Deyo (the old Basque name of this region). There is also the Romanesque church of San Andrés (Saint Andrew), which dates from the twelfth century. While the building is very interesting, the Baroque style of its bell tower is a little disconcerting. But, apart from admiring the architecture, be aware that for the next three hours you will be walking through bare, open country without any nucleus of population between here and Los Arcos. This is therefore a good time to rest, to have something to eat or to buy provisions, if necessary.

On leaving Villamayor you soon appreciate that this section is going to be rather monotonous. Although the trail leads slightly downward, the descent is barely perceptible most of the time and you may feel like you are walking on the flat. Twenty-five minutes out from Villamayor you reach the last fountain before Los Arcos. Make sure that your water bottle is full. At this point you will also see a sign with brief information on a place known as the Cueva de los Hombres Verdes (the Cave of the Green Men), which is close by. This is a burial place which has been dated at around 2000 BC. As it had been a copper mine, the human remains,

A not so innocent game

In many hostels pilgrims will find a *juego de la oca* (literally, 'the game of the goose', a traditional board game in which players advance by squares according to the throw of the dice) and may hear talk about its 'hidden messages'. According to certain opinions, this game actually embodies a secret code of the Knights Templar symbolizing the Way of Saint James, where the goal is Santiago de Compostela, square number 6 is Puente la Reina, the gaol is Burgos and the geese are the guards, as were the Templars themselves.

together with the pottery and other utensils left there, have a greenish hue as a result of the oxidation of the ore. Hence the name.

Archaeological excavation was undertaken by Dr Joan Maluquer towards the end of the 1950s. The remains which he found and classified may be seen, in part, at the Museum of Navarre.

For an hour and a half the landscape is dull, only broken up now and again by the odd industrial or agricultural shed. However, shortly before coming to the fourth hour of the walk you will at least find a bench on which to sit down. In this bare terrain it comes as quite a surprise. Subsequently you will see a sign which explains that the bench marks the ruins of the old church of Yániz. Three menhirs also used to stand here until they were uprooted in

Sansol viewed from Torres del Río

1959. Their whereabouts have been unknown ever since. Unfortunately, their disappearance destroyed the 'evidence' behind the legend that they were three maidens turned to stone when they failed to obey their mother's order to go to mass.

It will take a little over half an hour more to reach Los Arcos. You enter the town via what is described as a service area, although it is in fact nothing more than a garage which an enterprising citizen has turned into a refreshments shop, having realized that pilgrims arrive here thirsty and tired after a three-hour walk without shade.

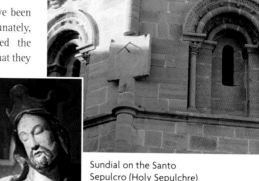

Sundial on the Santo Sepulcro (Holy Sepulchre) church at Torres del Río and the crowned Christ

Los Arcos – Sansol
6 h 10 min

Los Arcos was already an important point on the Way in medieval times and reference to it appears in the Codex Calixtinus of Aymeric Picaud. Even today you need only see the church of Santa María (Saint Mary) to appreciate the importance of the place.

Cross Los Arcos along the calle Mayor. On leaving it you will see a similar flat landscape. An hour later you cross a watercourse via a concrete ford and come to a sign explaining that this was the site of the old Melgán pilgrims' hospice. A little before reaching Sansol there is a stretch of road. The 500-metre walk through a cornfield is to be avoided, as the yellow arrows rightly indicate, because the ground there is soft and the going heavy.

Sansol – Torres del Río
6 h 30 min

Cross the town of Sansol and, following an easy descent, you will arrive at Torres del Río.

Eating
Stage 6 tends to be a very hot one and the terrain affords no shade. Therefore drink all you can and fill your water bottles systematically. There are shops for buying your provisions at Ayegui, Villamayor de Monjardín and Los Arcos. In the last two of these towns there are also bars where you can have a sandwich or a simple meal. At Torres del Río there is a shop where basic provisions may be obtained and a good restaurant.

Sleeping
There are three privately run hostels in Torres del Rio. Casa Mari (telephone 0034 948 648 409) is open all year. Mari, the owner, lives just half a dozen doors away on the same side of the street. This is useful to know if the hostel is closed at the time of your arrival. She does not serve dinner or breakfast, but the hostel does have some vending machines. There is also a place where pets can be housed. Casa Mariela (telephone 0034 948 648 251) was opened in the summer of 2009 and its installations are therefore practically new. It opens all year. Albergue La Pata de Oca (telephone 0034 948 378 457) likewise opens all year.

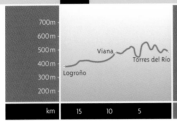

From Torres del Río to Logroño
Unexpected monuments

| km | 15 | 10 | 5 | 17.6 km • 4 h 55 min |

Torres del Río – Virgen del Poyo
40 min

Very few pilgrims will have heard of Torres del Río before coming to this part of the Way as it runs through Navarre. However, once having seen the town they will without doubt forever remember it as being one of the most surprising places on the whole of the pilgrimage. At first sight it could just be one more of those small urban communities which the Way passes through as it heads for La Rioja. When coming down from Sansol there is no reason to imagine that you are going to encounter a town which is in a constant process of urban restoration and provides, furthermore, a number of high-level services. It is, however, the Santo Sepulcro (Holy Sepulchre) church that will leave the visitor truly astounded.

Hidden away in the network of streets that runs up and down the hill, the church was built in the twelfth

The church of San Andrés (Saint Andrew) in Torres del Río

century and has an octagonal base. The doorway faces south. Its plan suggests that its origins lie with the Knights Templar, but no document has been found to support this theory. It is, on the other hand, obvious that its decoration has a Mudejar imprint and that there is a certain Cistercian air about it. The magnificence of the building lies in its simplicity. The nave is bare, without benches, and

Taking a rest at the Virgen del Poyo chapel. Right: grapes almost ready for harvesting

services are held with the congregation standing throughout.

The church has no fewer than fifty capitals decorated with flower and animal motifs. The most outstanding element, however, is the cupola. Eight arches rise from the corbels, their ribs intersecting to form a star. Openings at the base of the ribs provide the dome with natural light, displaying a clear Moorish influence. Advancing to the altar you will see the figure of a crowned Christ, unusual in that there are four nails, as the feet are separated, instead of the customary three. This confers a striking degree of realism on the scene.

The church is usually closed. In order to see the inside you need to call one of the women who look after the key (the telephone number appears on a notice pinned to the main door) and pay one euro.

With the image of the Santo Sepulcro still fresh in your minds, leave Torres del Río through the upper part of the town, following the yellow arrows which now take you past the parish church of San Andrés (Saint Andrew). Once out of the built-up area, you immediately come to an earth track. There are some sharp inclines, but they are not long enough to be tiring. If you have an altimeter to hand, you may see that you are, in general, gaining

Pilgrim on the path to Viana and (above) the town's entrance arch

height. After covering about two kilometres you reach the small church of the Virgen del Poyo. The construction remains solid, given that the church, originally built in the sixteenth century, has been restored on various occasions. Its rococo altarpiece is rated highly by the experts.

The temptations of La Rioja

Upon entering La Rioja the number of wineries beside the Way increases greatly. Although this is a temptation, bear in mind that to drink alcohol on a long walk is not to be recommended. Nor is it advisable to carry bottles, which are both heavy and fragile, in a backpack. However, why not try one of the region's other temptations, the red hot chilli peppers called alegrias. These may be bought in tiny cans and make a good souvenir.

Virgen del Poyo – Viana
2 h 35 min

This stretch calls for a certain patience, as it will be practically two hours before you reach the next centre of population – the only one you pass before reaching Logroño – and the track meanwhile rises and falls constantly. It is not tiring, however, as the slopes are short. The Mataburros gully constitutes the only variation. Once you have passed through that, go gently down to the historic town of Viana, a stronghold of the Way and once a bastion on the disputed frontier between the old kingdoms of Navarre and Castille.

The Baroque town hall is of interest, as is, particularly, the church of Santa María (Saint Mary), where Cesare Borgia, the son of Pope Alexander VI, is buried. He died in these parts at the beginning of the sixteenth century following a duel. The temple's Baroque altarpiece is alive with images.

It is worth taking a relaxing stroll around the old town before setting off once again.

Viana – Virgen de las Cuevas
3 h 20 min

The route out of the town is on well-marked, surfaced, local and secondary roads. After half an hour you

The sign marking the point where you leave Navarre and enter La Rioja and a ceramic plaque indicating the direction of the Way through the latter

come to a track which leads to the old chapel of Virgen de las Cuevas (Our Lady of the Caves). This cool, romantic place, with its shade and babbling stream, is an inviting spot for a picnic or siesta.

Virgen de las Cuevas – Logroño
4 h 55 min

This is not the prettiest section. Although you are following a path bordering a fragrant pine wood, the road, with its attendant noise, is very close by. The area where Navarre and La Rioja meet is one of the least interesting stretches of the Way. Eventually, you reach the outskirts of Logroño, where the only pleasant

The lively street Laurel in Logroño (left) and part of the wall

feature is the house of Doña Felisa, who used to stamp the pilgrims' passes and make them presents of fresh figs. Now her daughter, María, has taken over. Finally, you arrive at the downhill slope that takes you to the Puente de Piedra and the river Ebro, which mark the entrance to Logroño.

Eating
This stage is very short. Those who start out early will therefore reach Logroño in time for lunch and be able to spend the afternoon looking round the city. Those who prefer a slower pace, on the other hand, may choose to stay a little longer in Viana. It is the only point along the stage where provisions may be bought and there are, in addition, bars well stocked with

pintxos (as tapas are called in this part of Spain) and restaurants.

Sleeping
There is a very modern, large, well-equipped hostel (telephone 0034 941 248 686) in Logroño. It is run by the Asociación de Amigos del Camino and stands on Ruavieja, which you reach immediately after having crossed the Puente de Piedra over the Ebro.

It is open from March to October (from 15.00). The *hospitalero* usually makes pilgrims a gift of a little bottle of Rioja wine. In the old town there are half a dozen guest or boarding houses. These vary considerably in what they offer, but be prepared to pay 40 euros or more per night. The city also has a camping site called La Playa (telephone 0034 941 252 253) which is open all year.

Logroño
Tapas and wines around La Redonda

Co-cathedral of Santa María la Redonda

The church of Santa María (Saint Mary) la Redonda, a co-cathedral, dominates the old town, its twin towers reaching skywards. It is the city's largest church and dates from the fifteenth century. It has a Romanesque

doorway, shielded by wrought-iron railings. Inside there is a painting, attributed to Michelangelo, depicting the crucifixion. The towers have long been a favourite nesting place for storks, although some of these have recently been frightened off by ongoing works on the side of the building.

Ruavieja, along which the Way runs

The old town

In the old town of Logroño there are two streets in particular which the visitor cannot miss. The first, Portales, is full of traditional or more modern shops clustered under the arches which give the street its name. The local people have traditionally used it for their walks in winter, given the shelter that those arches provide. The second, Laurel, crammed with bars and taverns, is the favourite haunt of those delighting in tapas and wine. The alleyways running between the plaza del Mercado and the city hall are also worth seeing.

The Puente de Piedra over the river Ebro and (right) the façade of the co-cathedral at dusk.

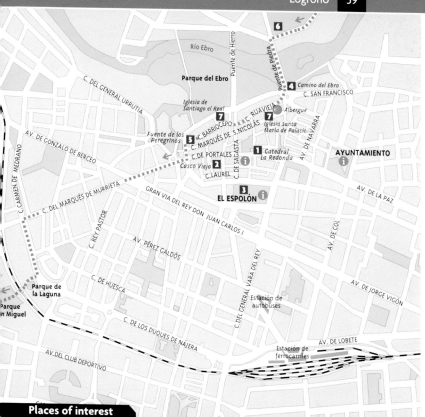

Río Ebro

C. DEL GENERAL URRUTIA

Parque del Ebro

Puente de Hierro

Puente de Piedra

4 Camino del Ebro
C. SAN FRANCISCO

AV. DE GONZALO DE BERCEO

Iglesia de
Santiago el Real
7

C. RUAVIEJA

Albergue

C. BARRIOCEPO

7

Iglesia Santa
María de Palacio

C. CARMEN DE MEDRANO

Fuente de los
Peregrinos

5 C. MARQUÉS DE S. NICOLÁS

C.DE PORTALES

Casco Viejo **2**

C.LAUREL

C. DE SAGASTA

1 Catedral
La Redonda

AV. DE NAVARRA

AYUNTAMIENTO

C. DEL MARQUÉS DE MURRIETA

GRAN VIA DEL REY DON JUAN CARLOS I

EL ESPOLÓN **3**

AV. DE LA PAZ

C. REY PASTOR

AV. PÉREZ GALDÓS

AV. DE COL

Parque de
la Laguna

Parque
n Miguel

C. DE HUESCA

C. DEL GENERAL VARA DEL REY

Estación de
autobuses

AV. DE JORGE VIGÓN

C. DE LOS DUQUES DE NÁJERA

AV. DE LOBETE

Estación de
ferrocarriles

AV.DEL CLUB DEPORTIVO

Places of interest

1 Co-cathedral
2 Old town
3 El Espolón park
4 Camino del Ebro
(riverside walk)
5 City walls and
Pilgrims' Fountain
6 Monument to the Way of
Saint James
7 Churches of Santa María de
Palacio and Santiago el Real

Eating

Logroño has a great deal to offer in this field, as the traveller will easily learn from a walk around the plaza del Mercado and its adjacent streets. Calles Portales and Laurel are famous for their wine and tapas bars. The local cookery is simple but tasty: lamb chops, sausage, peppers ...

Sleeping

The pilgrims' hostel run by the Asociación de Amigos del Camino (telephone 0034 941 248 686) is conveniently situated in Ruavieja and is modern and functional. It opens from March to October. The Puerta del Revellin hostel (telephone 0034 941 700 832) is in turn well equipped. A third hostel is the Parroquial de Santiago (no telephone), which opens from June to September. In the old town there are various other guest and boarding houses offering accommodation on good terms:
La Redonda
(telephone
0034 941 272 409)

at calle Portales. 21, Hostal Niza (telephone 0034 941 206 044) at calle Gallarza, 13, Huéspedes Villar (telephone 0034 941 220 228) at calle Martínez Zaporta, 7, Fonda la Bilbaina (telephone 0034 941 254 226) at calle Gallarza, 10, Hostal Sebastián (telephone 0034 941 242 800) at calle San Juan. 21, Hostal la Numantina (telephone 0034 941 251 411) at calle Sagasta, 4, Pensión Rey Pastor (telephone 0034 609 451 307) at calle Rey Pastor, 4 and many others at reasonable prices.

El Espolón

Paseo Principe de Vergara forms a park known as the Espolón which, they say in Logroño, is for the summer. Indeed, local people out for a walk in the evening, on Sundays or on public holidays have traditionally preferred calle Portales in the winter months, given the shelter it affords from the rain and cold, leaving this park for the summer evenings. This never fails to surprise visitors, once they realize that the two avenues are barely 200 metres apart. Today the Espolón, with its gardens and statue of General Baldomero Fernández Espartero on horseback, is an oasis of fountains and shade, where concerts are held on many summer nights on the stage erected on the west side.

Bridges over the Ebro and riverside walk

The river Ebro has played a key role in the history and development of the city. The view of the river is at its best in the evening, when the lighting is on, from the south bank.

The Puente de Piedra is a work of engineering in which, it is said, the saints Domingo de la Calzada (Dominic of the Causeway) and Juan de Ortega (John the Hermit), no less, were involved. It is, at all events, a true pleasure to walk by the riverbank and to cross the Ebro by way of that bridge or any of the

Plaza de San Agustín in summer (top) and a bar in calle Laurel. Below: the statue of Espartero.

others: Mantible, Sagasta, de Hierro or the footbridge. A new infrastructure, the GR-99, also now passes through this area. The GR-99 is a path, recently restored and marked, running for almost 1,300 km beside the river. The Logroño stretch, marked with red and white stripes, enters via the Cortijo quarter and subsequently moves on towards the neighbouring town of Agoncillo. It provides a perfect view of the islets in the river and the birds which inhabit the banks.

City walls and Pilgrims' Fountain

Pilgrims most often stay at the hostel in Ruavieja, which they come to upon entering the city. On the following morning they continue along that same street on their way out. At a certain point they come to the Pilgrims' Fountain, where they may stop for water. You don't need much imagination to picture the thousands of pilgrims who have, over the centuries, descended the steps to that fountain in order to fill their water bottles or, formerly, gourds. The Puerta del Camino gateway marks the exit from the city.

Churches of Santa María de Palacio and Santiago el Real

These are the two churches of which the citizens of Logroño are most proud. That of Santa María (Saint Mary) de Palacio is distinctive in that its pyramid-shaped tower, known locally as La Aguja (the needle), is a feature of the city's skyline. The church dates from the eleventh and twelfth centuries. The doorway of the church of Santiago (Saint James) el Real bears an image of Saint James the Moor-slayer. It is not to be forgotten that Clavijo, the site of the battle where the saint intervened so decisively, is very close to Logroño.

The Pilgrims' Fountain and the church of Santiago el Real. Below, María stamping passes and offering fresh figs.

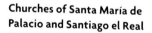

Monument to the Way

On entering La Rioja travellers are for a while brought into unwelcome contact with tarmacked roads and disconcerting junctions which jar with the tranquillity of the experience so far. However, upon reaching the monument to the Way of Saint James they are rewarded with a vision of Logroño reflected in the waters of the Ebro. The monument combines both avant-garde and traditional styles and is not to everyone's taste, but it is without doubt one of the most original along the entire pilgrimage route.

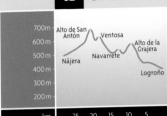

From Logroño to Nájera
Vineyard upon vineyard

700m
600m
500m
400m
300m
200m

Alto de San Antón
Ventosa
Alto de la Grajera
Nájera
Navarrete
Logroño

km   25   20   15   10   5

28.9 km • 7 h

Logroño – Alto de la Grajera
2 h 10 min

On leaving the hostel in Logroño continue along Ruavieja and then take calle Barriocepo, following the arrows. Soon you come to the Pilgrim's Fountain, set a little below the level of the street. In accordance with tradition, go down the steps to that fountain and fill your water bottles, just as millions of other travellers have done in the course of the centuries. On the right side of the street is the imposing church of Santiago el Real and, if you pay attention, you will notice that the paving of the plaza de Santiago is inset with a giant *juego de la oca*, a game closely associated with the Way (see page 52).

After passing through the gateway in the walls you come to an

Chozo (stone hut) near Poyo de Roldán

area of gardens with a roundabout which is a little confusing. However, continue to head south-west and you come to the broad Marqués de Murrieta avenue, which you will be following for a good while.

The city stretches into outskirts and you have to walk for some time before crossing the railway line and coming to a corner (calle Portillejo) where various car dealerships are situated. Here turn left, leaving behind

Bridge over the La Grajera reservoir, just out of Logroño

Nájera | 2h 25 min | Ventosa | 1h 40 min | Navarrete | 45h | Alto de La Grajera | 2h 10 min | **Logroño** ←

the sounds of the city, and follow a bicycle lane which immediately takes you to an underpass under the motorway. Fifty-five minutes have gone by since the starting point. Once the noise of the traffic fades into the distance, you'll hear nothing more than birdsong and the rustling tracksuits of those who like to train in this parkland.

The walk through the parkland is very pleasant. You come to the La Grajera reservoir, protected by a low wall, and, following a well-marked path, you reach the bridge that takes you over a corner of the reservoir. Waterfowl abound in this area.

Once over the bridge you come to a steady but not particularly demanding climb up a concrete track, leading between picnic and other leisure facilities. It will take almost an hour to cover this stretch. Kiosks, usually open in the summer season alone, are to be found from time to time and you may therefore get the chance to stop for a coffee.

After rounding a sharp bend you reach Alto de la Grajera, which has a wire fence to which pilgrims have affixed little crosses made from toothpicks. The motorway is now below you and once again you will hear the roar of vehicles.

The old town of Navarrete

Alto de la Grajera – Navarrete
2 h 55 min

Following a brief rest on the hill, with its pleasant oaks and holm oaks, begin a long descent along paths that are generally well surfaced, running between vineyards, to Navarrete. First you will see the ruins of the hospice of San Juan de Acre (see box on the next page) and then come to the town, where it is worth allowing yourself a little

time to look around. The old town is full of streets with imposing houses. One of these is calle Mayor, along which the Way runs. Others include calle Nueva, with its arches, and Cuesta del Caño.

Navarrete is well known for its pottery and in the square by the church there is a monument which pays tribute to the potter's art. About a dozen potteries are currently open to the public and in them you can see clay being worked in the traditional manner. You can also buy finished products, but since the material is both fragile and heavy this is not such a good idea while walking the Way

However, you might be able to find something small and therefore portable.

In terms of monuments, a visit to the parish church of la Asunción

(the Assumption), which dates from the sixteenth century, is recommended. Navarrete does not forget how important the Way has been for the town historically. Thus, every 25 July the association of local townswomen organizes a musical evening to which pilgrims are expressly invited. There is also a charming monument to the travellers who pass through on their way to Santiago.

Ruins of San Juan de Acre
The ruins of the monastery of San Juan de Acre lie just a few hundred metres outside the town of Navarrete. Founded in 1185, it used to be a pilgrims' hospice. Today all that remains is the base of some of the principal walls, but information panels have been erected so that the traveller may appreciate the importance that the site once had within the history of the Way.

Navarrete – Ventosa
4 h 35 min
Leaving Navarrete, you will see the cemetery to your left. Its size is striking and so is its impressive Gothic gateway. This used, in fact, to be the entrance to the old hospice of San Juan de Acre before it was brought here. It is richly ornamented and its geometrical figures stand out. On an adjacent wall you can see a plaque to the memory of a cyclist pilgrim killed in an accident in 1986.

The walk from here to Ventosa takes little more than half an hour. The Way follows secondary roads and runs between vineyards. There is very little traffic, but precisely for that reason be careful not to become complacent about it.

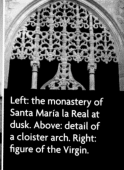

Left: the monastery of Santa María la Real at dusk. Above: detail of a cloister arch. Right: figure of the Virgin.

Ventosa – Alto de San Antón
5 h

Between Navarrete and Alto de San Antón there is a short but very stiff climb. The shelter hitherto provided by the vineyards wanes at this point and the wind can often be troublesome. The good thing, however, is that when you reach the top you can see Nájera, no more than some eight kilometres away, and that the rest of the stage is all downhill.

Alto de San Antón – Nájera
7 h

The last two hours of the stage are a little monotonous, with only vines for company, although you will pass a reconstructed *chozo* – a stone hut traditionally used locally for storing agricultural implements and similar purposes – near Poyo de Roldán, where the legendary warrior defeated the giant Ferragut.

Farther on the path passes by an aggregates quarry and the landscape suffers as a result. Although on approaching Nájera a series of bucolic little bridges spanning streams are visible, the scene is marred by occasional mounds of rubble. Finally, you will walk through the new part of the town, cross the river Najerilla and reach the hostel.

Eating

This stage is quite a long one and does not go through many towns. However, in Navarrete and Ventosa there are bars, restaurants and grocery shops. There is also a kiosk in the park of La Grajera, at the beginning of the stage. The most attractive option on a pleasant day may be to put some food and drink in your backpack and then have a picnic in the shade of a vine.

Sleeping

There are two hostels in Nájera. One stands by the river Najerilla, is open all year and is run by the Asociación de Amigos del Camino. It does not have a telephone. The *hospitalero* does his best to make the sober facilities provided by the one-storey house as comfortable as possible. The Sancho III hostel (telephone 0034 941 361 138) opens from Holy Week to October. Couples desiring privacy may ask for a double room, although in that event they will have to be prepared to pay boarding house rates.

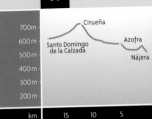

From Nájera to Santo Domingo de la Calzada
A day of monuments

18.3 km • 5 h

Nájera – Azofra
1 h 20 min

The monastery of Santa María la Real (Royal Saint Mary) is the pride of Nájera and one of the most beautiful buildings on the entire Way. It warrants more than a cursory visit. The traveller enters through the Carlos I doorway, which leads direct to the cloister of the Caballeros (knights), so called because its walls house the tombs of numerous Riojan and Basque nobles who mostly lived between the sixteenth and eighteenth centuries. One of the most important is the mausoleum of Diego López de Haro, lord of Bizkaia in the thirteenth century and founder of the city of Bilbao. The traceries of the arches are magnificent, resembling crochet work in stone, and each one different.

Once inside the monastery, the architectural style you can see is late Gothic with some Plateresque additions, such as the galleries. The royal pantheon, dating from around 1556, houses the tombs of some of the monarchs of Navarre of the Jimena or Abarca dynasties and that of King García Ramírez the Restorer.

In the crypt there is a cave where the Gothic figure of the Virgen de la Rosa (Our Lady of the Rose) may be seen. According to legend, the image was found in this precise spot by a noble falconer out hunting for partridge. A monastery was then founded on the spot,

Historic monasteries

Thousands of pilgrims have, over the years, made a detour in order to visit the nearby monasteries at San Millán de la Cogolla. In that of Suso, which is troglodytic, lie the remains of San Millán (Saint Emilianus). That of Yuso has one of the most beautiful sacristies in the whole peninsula. The twin monasteries have been a World Heritage site since 1997.

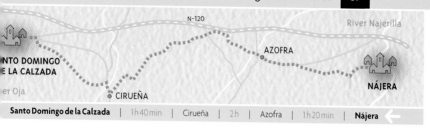

Santo Domingo de la Calzada | 1h40min | Cirueña | 2h | Azofra | 1h20min | **Nájera**

together with a pilgrims' hospice of which nothing remains.

You also have to see the pantheon of the infantes, where the most famous tomb is that of Blanca of Navarre with its decorated sarcophagus, and the choir stalls. The ornate carving is a masterpiece of the florid Gothic style of the late fifteenth century, full of monsters and demons, of religious, geometrical and plant motifs and of scenes from the everyday life of the time.

Lastly, there is the great Baroque reredos of the main altar, depicting the Virgin with the child Jesus blessing the people.

Still marvelling at the beauty of the monastery, follow the yellow arrows out of Nájera. You will pass close by some old cave dwellings dug out of the soft rock of the outcrops to the north of the town.

The Way is well marked and runs along trails through

agricultural land. This stretch is rather monotonous and flat, except at the beginning where there is a steep slope about a kilometre in length. To the south you can see the Ezcaray mountains on the horizon. Snow generally remains on their peaks until well into the year. The approach to Azofra is slightly uphill, but the ascent is barely perceptible.

The long descent towards Santo Domingo

Azofra – Crucero (wayside cross)
1 h 40 min

Today Azofra is a small place, walked across in very little time. However, the ancestral houses on its calle Mayor, along which you will walk from end to end, bear witness to the importance that the town has had over the centuries. In the square there is a fountain with four jets where you might pause for a moment but only to freshen up since, as a notice points out, the water is not drinkable. You may also take a look at the parish church, where there is a statue of Santiago Peregrino (Saint James the Pilgrim).

The cock and the hen waiting for the works on the cathedral to finish

Finding the route out of the town can prove a little difficult, as the arrows have rather worn away. However, soon you will find yourself on a broad, gravel, forest track. For about two hours the route goes gradually upward, although the ascent is barely perceptible, until you come to the turnoff to San Millán de Cogolla (although the sign says Alesanco).

Some twenty minutes out from Azofra there is a medieval cross which was formerly a *picota*, a stone column to which wrongdoers were shackled, by way of a lesson, and where the heads of executed criminals were exhibited.

Crucero – Cirueña
3 h 20 min

Leaving the cross behind, move on towards Cirueña. This is a straightforward stretch of a couple of hours on which one of the nicer distractions is

The Plaza Mayor (main square) and town hall of Santo Domingo seen from the cathedral tower

observing the flight of storks or other birds common to this region. When you reach the outskirts of the town, however, some recently built developments show you the impact that the golf course has had. The old town lies to the right of the Way and does not contain many buildings of note. There is no need to visit it, unless you simply wish to take a look around.

Cirueña – Santo Domingo de la Calzada

5 h

Five minutes out from Cirueña you come to the high point of the stage at a little more than 700 m above sea level. From here you can see the outline of Santo Domingo de la Calzada just eight kilometres away.

Continue along the same broad, straight track. Although the going is easy, there is no shade. All you can see is the occasional cairn left by pilgrims and some handmade crosses. As you enter Santo Domingo you may notice that the transition from country to city is smooth and clean, without the intermediate waste ground which is all too common elsewhere. Go along the calle Mayor and past the Centro de Interpretación del Camino de Santiago (Way of Saint James Interpretation Centre), characterized by a display of technical wizardry and a rather over-the-top theatricality intended to help the tourist feel the sensations of the pilgrim. Although admission is free for those in possession of a pilgrim's pass, true pilgrims do not seem to need the virtual; they are living the reality. Within the town take care not to lose the way, as the yellow arrows are not visible at times.

Façade and tower of the cathedral

Eating

This is a short stage which passes through no more than a couple of towns. Both Azofra and Cirueña have grocery shops and bars, but in the winter months pilgrims may find little or nothing open if they come through early in the morning. The route is also very exposed. There is practically no shade, nor is there anywhere to take shelter in the event of bad weather.

Sleeping

There are two hostels in Santo Domingo, both in the calle Mayor. The Anunciación hostel (telephone 0034 941 340 570) is Cistercian and opens from June to September. Casa del Santo (telephone 0034 941 343 390) is open all year. There are also numerous guest and boarding houses offering accommodation at a range of prices.

900 m
800 m — Villamayor
del Río
700 m — Belorado   Castildelgado
600 m   Grañón
500 m   Santo Domingo
400 m   de la Calzada

km   15   10   5

From Santo Domingo de la Calzada to Belorado
Entrada en Castilla

19.9 km • 5 h 40 min

Santo Domingo de la Calzada – Grañón
1 h 40 min

Known as 'the Compostela of Rioja', Santo Domingo de la Calzada is so closely linked to the Way and has so many monuments that a full visit is warranted. The old town is shady and pleasant. Centred around the calle Mayor, by which you enter the city, it has an array of imposing houses bearing witness to the antiquity and nobility of the place. You will also find the modern, interactive Way of Saint James Interpretation Centre here. This is of greater interest to the tourist than to the pilgrim, who is already experiencing the sensations of the pilgrimage in person. However, in order to get in free you get a pilgrim's pass. Otherwise there is a charge of ten euros.

Plaza Mayor (main square) of Santo Domingo de la Calzada

The city's most outstanding building is without doubt the cathedral. Inside is the famous coop housing the cock and hen which symbolize the legend associated with the city (see box on next page). Construction of the cathedral commenced in the twelfth century, precisely so that it could be the burial place of Saint Dominic. The main altarpiece, the choir, the saint's sepulchre and the chicken coop are four of the elements of most interest for the tourist.

Visitors may climb the cathedral tower, which is separate from the main building, and thus enjoy an excellent view of the plaza Mayor, a large part of the old town and the fields round about. Admission is 1.5 euros.

Gateway of the church in Grañón and image of a pilgrim on the town's coat of arms

From Santo Domingo de la Calzada to Belorado

BURGOS | LA RIOJA

River Villar

SANTO DOMINGO DE LA CALZADA

-ORADO | VILLAMAYOR DEL RÍO | N-120 | REDECILLA DEL CAMINO

N-120

VILORIA DE RIOJA | CASTILDELGADO | GRAÑÓN

ver Tirón

River Oja

Belorado | 2 h | Viloria | 1 h | Redecilla del Camino | 1 h | Grañón | 1 h 40 min | **Santo Domingo de la Calzada**

Your visit may also take in, first, the plaza Mayor, where the town hall stands. The sides of the open square feature the typical arches so frequently to be seen throughout Castile. The walls of the city are the biggest in the whole of La Rioja and date from the fourteenth century. The bridge over the river Oja was the scene of various miracles performed by Saint Dominic. In the most famous he brought a young man who had been run over by a cart back to life. Lastly, there are two convents, that of San Francisco (Saint Francis), which now shares its extensive facilities with a *parador* (a state-run luxury hotel), a workshop where works of art are restored and a hospital, and the Cistercian nuns' abbey, dating from the seventeenth century.

From the cathedral the yellow arrows guide you out of Santo Domingo and lead once again to

Pilgrims advancing from La Rioja into the province of Burgos

earth tracks flanked by cornfields which in spring are green, in the early summer are yellow and in winter are the ochre of the dormant earth. The next town on the route is Grañón.

A hen with a grip on life

This local legend is so well known that the saying 'where the hen sang after being roasted' is even recorded as the town hall motto. When a young pilgrim was wrongly sentenced to be hanged for a theft he had not committed, Saint Dominic worked a miracle whereby a hen which had already been roasted rose and began to sing in proof of the innocence of the boy, whose life was thus saved.

Grañón – Redecilla del Camino
2 h 40 min

A good, broad track leads, in gentle ascent through terrain practically devoid of shade, to Grañón, which you enter via its long calle Mayor. This town, which has plenty of facilities, is the last in the autonomous community of La Rioja, as you will be informed not long after leaving it.

The terrain remains exactly the same, but the regional authorities ensure that you are aware of the boundaries. Thus, on a small bend to the right you come to a huge metal sign marking the starting point of the province of Burgos and, therefore, of the autonomous community of Castilla y León. There is also a panel with a map on which you can take an advance look at the stages you will be covering in the coming weeks, as it shows the entire course of the Way through this historic region. On this stretch the pedestrian suffers a little on the bare, shadeless track. The cyclist, in contrast, can take advantage of the level terrain to keep up a steady speed.

Pilgrims in large numbers in the summer

Redecilla del Camino – Castildelgado
3 h 5 min

Shortly after entering the province of Burgos you come to the town of Redecilla del Camino. Cross the road here, taking even more care than usual because the monotony of the landscape may have dulled your senses a little, and you come to a little square where a fountain provides refreshment. Although small, the town has good facilities and therefore warrants consideration as a place to stop for lunch, bearing in mind, furthermore, that you have by now covered more than half the day's journey. It is a good idea to have a rest here, given that in the course of the last three kilometres you have climbed over a hundred metres and that the stretch which lies ahead in turn has steep inclines and is therefore no less tough.

Castildelgado – Viloria
3 h 40 min

Even at the speed of the foot pilgrim, so small is

Arriving at Redecilla del Camino

the village of Castildelgado that it seems to go by in a flash. The trail continues to climb until it takes you to Viloria. The town is small but famous in the area because it is the birthplace of Saint Dominic. The church houses the font where the saint was baptized in the year 1019, but at the time of writing it was closed to visitors pending completion of the restoration work to the building.

Viloria – Villamayor del Río
4 h 25 min

Leave Viloria on a surfaced road which leads gently downward for some time, then link up with a path running parallel to the main road. This takes you to Villamayor del Río, which is quickly crossed.

Villamayor del Río – Belorado
5 h 40 min

A rural track leads, descending little by little, to Belorado, where you come to the first hostel before entering the town as such. On completing this stage take note (as your legs already may have done) that you have now covered a third of the Way.

Church (above) and bandstand in the centre of Belorado

Eating
This stage poses no difficulty as regards the availability of shops, bars and restaurants. All the towns you pass through have these facilities and it is therefore by no means essential that you carry provisions in your packs. In the winter season some of those facilities may be closed or have limited opening hours, but there are so many of them that this is not a problem.

Sleeping
There are no fewer than five pilgrims' hostels in Belorado: A Santiago (telephone 0034 677 811 847), Parroquial (Parish) (telephone 0034 947 580 085), Caminante (telephone 0034 656 873 927), El Corro (telephone 0034 670 691 173) and Cuatro Cantones (telephone 0034 696 427 707). There are also a youth hostel, a hotel and various boarding houses.

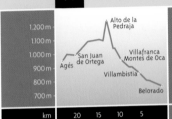

From Belorado to Agés
Montes de Oca

23 km • 6 h 15 min

Belorado – Tosantos
1 h

The walk from Belorado is on easy, level ground beside the road. The landscape at once takes on the familiar look of these past days: a rural track with cornfields on either side. After a few minutes the path starts to become steep, little by little at first, for about twenty minutes. You then come once again to level terrain until you reach Tosantos, which is small but has a bar and a hostel.

Bridge at Villambistia

Tosantos – Villambistia
1 h 25 min

From Tosantos you can see the chapel of the Virgen de la Peña (Our Lady of the Rock), clinging to a wall of rock. The path runs along the back of the town and then out towards Villambistia, whose church you can see in the distance. Now the path ascends quite steeply and continues thus for a good part of the day as this stage includes going over the Montes de Oca hills.

If it is open, the church of San Esteban (Saint Steven) at Villambistia is worth a visit. It looks like an impregnable stronghold. Inside the village you will pass by a pretty octagonal fountain with four jets surmounted by a wrought-iron cross. This used to be the source of the water supply for the villagers, but now its water is not drinkable.

The route out of Villambistia is along a broad, smooth, rural track.

Villambistia – Espinosa del Camino
1 h 50 min

Although it becomes progressively steeper, the track will take you to the next town, Espinosa del Camino, in less than half an hour. The name of the

Ruins of the monastery of San Felices (Saint Felix) beside a stone Way marker

SAN JUAN DE ORTEGA — Arroyo de San Juan — River Cerrata de la Pedraja — ESPINOSA DEL CAMINO — TOSANTOS — BELORADO — Vera — Alto de La Pedraja 1.250 m — N-120 — VILLAFRANCA MONTES DE OCA — N-120 — VILLAMBISTIA — River Oca — River Tirón

Agés | 50 min | San Juan de Ortega | 2 h 45 min | Villafranca de Montes de Oca | 1 h 40 min | Tosantos | 1 h | **Belorado**

Ascent to Alto de la Pedraja. Below: pilgrims in Villafranca.

town suggests that it grew up precisely as a result of the passage of pilgrims. Today it still has a hostel, but the rest of the town's business seems to be failing. And many of its houses look neglected and almost abandoned. On leaving Espinosa you face the longest and steepest part of the day's route. Over the next five kilometres you will ascend by 200 m. Before that, however, you come to the ruins of the monastery of San Felices or San Félix. These stand very close to the side of the track and are identified by a sign.

Espinosa del Camino – Monasterio de San Felices
2 h 15 min

From the ruins of the monastery you can work out that you are looking at the area where the main altar and the apse were situated. According to the history books, the founder of the city of Burgos, Diego Porcelos, may have been buried here.

Monasterio de San Felices – Villafranca de Montes de Oca
2 h 40 min

Leaving the monastery behind, cross the river Oca and then continue on, walking uncomfortably close to the road. Be careful because the traffic is rather heavy on this stretch.

The town of Villafranca, whose church is dedicated to Saint James, must have known better days, to judge by its current look. As it is the last populated place you will pass through before reaching San Juan de Ortega, this is an appropriate moment to buy provisions, if necessary, or to stop for lunch, bearing in mind that you have covered half of the day's journey. From here you enter the oak woods of Montes de Oca, where there are no facilities of any kind.

Villafranca de Montes de Oca – Alto de la Pedraja
3 h 30 min

Following a gentle ascent lasting just ten minutes, the path again starts to climb steeply. You will reach a viewpoint facing the San Millán mountains where there are benches where you can rest. This is a very good idea, as the steepest stretch now lies ahead. The track is broad and smooth and you walk through a good-sized oak wood, dotted here and there with ash and juniper. It is the first wooded area of any size that you will have seen since leaving Navarre. It will, however, also be the last you'll see in many days, for the rest of the route through Castile is practically devoid of trees.

Coming to Alto de la Pedraja, at

Impressive monuments

San Juan de Ortega is just a small village within the municipality of Barrios de Colinas. However, such was its importance, historically, on the Way of Saint James that it boasts a magnificent array of monuments including the group formed by the church, the chapel of San Nicolás de Bari (Saint Nicholas), the Hieronymite monastery and the building which is now the pilgrims' hostel.

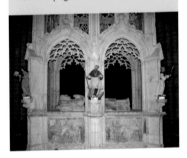

1,250 m above sea level, you will see that the monument to the memory of Civil War dead, erected here some decades ago, remains, almost surprisingly, undamaged. Close beside it there is a picnic area (Valbuena) with stone tables and benches at which you can rest. From here there is a good view of the valley below. Although you won't have to walk along it, the road runs close by and you will constantly hear the hum of the traffic.

Alto de la Pedraja – San Juan de Ortega
5 h 25 min

You now come to a series of steep inclines, although the overall trend is downward, on a

San Juan de Ortega

stretch that will take almost two hours to cover. The trail runs through an area of deforestation that is frankly ugly. The path is in a very poor state and littered with the debris of the extraction process, while heavy vehicles manoeuvre to carry the timber out.

Fountain at the entrance to the village of Agés

San Juan de Ortega – Agés

6 h 15 min

San Juan de Ortega is worth a leisurely visit. Start by going to the church to admire the capital where the 'miracle of light' occurs on the days of the spring and autumn equinoxes (21 March and 22 September). On those days a ray of light enters the building and illuminates the image of the Annunciation, in which the Archangel Gabriel and the Virgin Mary may be seen. The mausoleum of Saint John, with the canopy that surrounds it, the chapel of San Nicolás de Bari (Saint Nicholas) and the building that is now the pilgrims' hostel are all worth visiting too. The hostel was recently renovated and the inadequacies which so many pilgrims had previously suffered have now been fixed. The sanctuary as a whole has national monument status. Beside the hostel stands Casa Marcela, a bar where it is traditional to eat black pudding with fried eggs.

From San Juan de Ortega to Agés there is a pleasant walk of three quarters of an hour through an oak wood.

Eating
You need to eat and buy food and water on the first half of this stage. In Tosantos, Espinosa and Villafranca there are bars and restaurants and the last two also have shops. After crossing the river Oca, however, there is nowhere to buy anything until you reach San Juan de Ortega.

Sleeping
There are four hostels in Agés but one of them, Casa Caracol (telephone 0034 947 430 413), was closed at the time of writing. The municipal

hostel (telephone 0034 947 400 697) opens all year round. San Rafael (telephone 0034 947 430 392) similarly opens all year and has, in addition to the usual bunk beds, a few double rooms (available for a higher price obviously). Pajar de Agés (telephone 0034 947 400 629) opens from March to October.

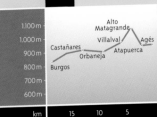

From Agés to Burgos
An urban slog

Alto
Matagrande
Villalval   Agés
Castañares   Atapuerca
Orbaneja
Burgos

1.100 m
1.000 m
900 m
800 m
700 m
600 m

km   15   10   5

18.9 km • 5 h 10 min

Agés – Atapuerca
35 min

Agés is a small but pretty town and a pleasant place to take a stroll. In the old quarter there are houses in a traditional style of architecture which you will be seeing progressively more of as the day goes on. Wood and adobe (sun-dried clay and straw bricks) are the basic elements of construction, although you will see that stone also has a role to play in the local architecture. There are a couple of fountains with granite basins, the old public laundry and, particularly, the single-arched Roman bridge with its impressive cutwater on the river Vena. Although it generally appears to be little more than a stream, when full the Vena can cause severe flooding even in the city of Burgos, or so the local people say. The church is also worth a visit.

The first section of the

The church at Agés

stage leads slightly downhill, along a road with very little traffic, to Atapuerca. You may want to go into the centre of the town, but the path takes you lower down, then to the left past the monument to the ancestor and out of the town. Atapuerca has become world famous for its palaeontological sites, chief among which is the Sima de los Huesos (the pit of bones), where the remains of some of the human race's earliest forebears have been found. Unfortunately, however, the sites are three kilometres off the Way. The return trip, plus the time

Sign and monument
at the Atapuerca
archaeological sites

| Burgos | 2h35min | Orbaneja | 55min | Villalbal | 1h5min | Atapuerca | 35min | **Agés** |

spent at the sites, would take up a large part of the day.

Atapuerca – Villalbal
1 h 40 min
Leave Atapuerca along a broad, stony track which takes you steadily upward to an unnamed hill where, from a height of 1,050 m, you may see, first of all, the sparse oak wood through which you will descend towards the next town. Beyond it you will also see the broad plain of Burgos and, in the distance, the towers of the city's cathedral. You can thus roughly estimate the distance you still have to cover on this stage. Leaving this windy spot behind, move sharply downward between the trees along an awkward path strewn with large stones, and you come to Villalbal. The town has no facilities or buildings of note so cross it without stopping.

Villalbal – Cardeñuela-Río Pico
2 h 5 min
Descending little by little, the path leads in about thirty minutes to Cardeñuela-Río Pico, a village consisting of little more than a single street along which the Way runs. There is a bar and a pilgrims' hostel, but it is better to wait until you reach Orbaneja, which is barely thirty minutes away, before stopping.

A field of sunflowers in summer

Graffiti on a wall in Atapuerca

Cardeñuela-Río Pico – Orbaneja
2 h 35 min

This stretch takes you along a local road with no hard shoulder but likewise, fortunately, practically no traffic. It is flat and therefore allows you to reach Orbaneja with fairly little effort. Once in the town it may be a good idea to stop at a bar, study the map and perhaps seek the views of the local people as to the alternatives there might be for eating and drinking.

Orbaneja – Castañares
3 h 35 min

Of the many stages of the Way of Saint James, this is the one that will probably cause you most headaches. You will probably have heard experienced walkers, who have travelled the Way before, say that the approach to Burgos is the least pleasant and most tiring stretch on the entire pilgrimage. There are, in fact, two routes leading to the city, but neither of them is enticing. The traditional route, which most pilgrims follow, goes from Orbaneja

The grapevine of the Way
There is plenty of time to chat while walking or at the hostel and thus to keep a secret for the length of the pilgrimage is quite difficult. News travels fast and, as a result, everybody knows that a certain Dutch girl is undertaking the pilgrimage after having been disappointed in love, that the chap from Valencia works for the gas company and that the bearded Austrian is partial to brandy. Be careful what you tell people.

to Villafría along a local road but then, from Villafría, runs along the main N-1, where the vehicles roar by unpleasantly and, at times, dangerously close. This stretch is laborious. The noise is hellish and, although you are walking on the flat, the kilometres

Pilgrims about to enter Burgos.
Right: the river Arlanzón.

seem double their normal length. A few years ago an alternative route was opened up. It does not afford any great improvement as regards landscape, nor is it a short cut, but it is certainly quieter and, above all, safer, as you avoid having to walk near to the traffic and to negotiate dangerous crossings. This is, therefore, definitely the recommended route.

On leaving Orbaneja cross a bridge over the N-1 motorway and you come to a small development with white houses. To the left you'll see the yellow arrows. Following these down a muddy slope, round the development and towards the aerodrome. Here you have to walk beside the perimeter fence. There aren't many signs, but there is no risk of losing the way. You then pass by an area of waste ground strewn with rubble. Here, again, you momentarily lose sight of the arrows, but the direction you should take is obvious, and leads straight to the town of Castañares.

Castañares – Burgos
5 h 10 min

The landscape may not be any better, but this is a much easier route. It is a long pathway running between milestones, a boring, 10-km stretch through an industrial area. However, although it is dull be aware that there is a lot of heavy traffic going in and out of the factories.

After crossing the railway lines you come to a large roundabout. Take calle Vitoria and enter the city.

Façade of Burgos cathedral

Eating
With the exception of Villalbal, all the towns or villages you go through on this stage have a restaurant or, at least, a bar, although in the low season some of these may open late or may simply be closed. There are, however, no shops in the towns preceding Castañares. Fortunately, the stage is fairly short.

Sleeping
Burgos offers a broad range of possibilities. The municipal hostel, El Cubo (telephone 0034 947 460 922), is beside the cathedral and is open all year. Aside from this there are privately-run hostels. That of Santiago y Santa Catalina (telephone 0034 947 207 952) opens from March to November; that of Emaús (no telephone) opens from April to November. The Divina Pastora (telephone 0034 947 207 952) opens from Holy Week to mid-October. A youth hostel (telephone 0034 947 220 362) is also available in the summer. For those who prefer more privacy there are likewise many guest and boarding houses.

Burgos
A cathedral reborn

Distance
behind you
246.8 km

Cathedral

Work on the construction of Burgos cathedral began in 1221. In recent years the building has undergone in-depth restoration. Its two towers, dominating plaza de Santa María, are very impressive. Having admired the imposing exterior, the visitor really needs a number of hours to appreciate the marvels inside. There is the golden stairway, in Italian Renaissance style, the central nave and the chapel of San Nicolás (Saint Nicholas), which has a thirteenth-century altar and a still older Romanesque sepulchre. In the area devoted to worship and prayer we find the chapel of the Santísimo Cristo de Burgos (Most Holy Christ of Burgos), with a fourteenth-century carving and the sixteenth-century clock known as *Papamoscas* (flycatcher), and the Baroque style chapel of Santa Tecla (Saint Thecla).

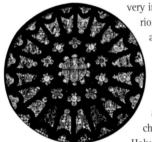

Rose window of the cathedral

In the central nave you will notice the sepulchre of El Cid and Doña Jimena, as well as the main altarpiece and the choir. But it is in the chapel of the Condestables (the Constables) where tourists are most often left open-mouthed. There, in addition to the sepulchre (see box on page 85), admire the central altarpiece, the starred vault, the painting of Mary Magdalene by Giampetrino and the canvas representing Christ crucified.

Above: detail of the cathedral.
Right: arch of Santa María.

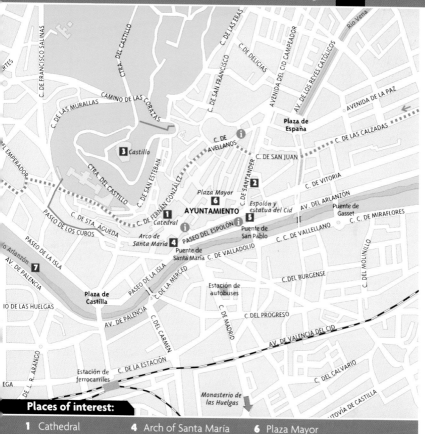

Places of interest:

1 Cathedral
2 Casa del Cordón
3 El Castillo park

4 Arch of Santa María
5 Espolón and statue
  of El Cid

6 Plaza Mayor
7 River Arlanzón
8 Las Huelgas monastery

Eating

Throughout the old town numerous tapas bars and restaurants offer food at a wide range of prices. Some are famous for their meat: Mesón de los Infantes at paseo de la Isla, 2 (telephone 0034 947 279 542), Casa Ojeda at calle Vitoria, 5 (telephone 0034 947 209 052) or Vinoteca Cordón at calle Puebla. 3 (telephone 0034 947 277 279).

There are shops and bakeries in the area around

the plaza Mayor where pilgrims may buy supplies.

Sleeping

Aside from the hostels, there are guest and boarding houses around the plaza Mayor and in the old town which offer accommodation at affordable prices. They include Pensión Peña at calle Puebla, 18 (telephone 0034 947 206 323), Pensión Victoria at calle San Juan, 3 (telephone 0034 947 201 542), Hostal Acacia at calle Peréz Ortíz, 1 (telephone

0034 947 205 134) and Hostal Liar at calle Cardenal Belloch (telephone 0034 947 209 655). If you want to treat yourself to a hotel with views of the cathedral, Hotel Mesón del Cid at plaza Santa María, 8 (telephone 0034 947 203 049) has a good reputation. Lastly, there is the Fuentes Blancas camp site (telephone 0034 947 486 016). At four kilometres from the city it is a little out of the way, but there are buses which stop right outside.

Monument to the pilgrim and details of the cathedral. On the next page: statue of El Cid.

Casa del Cordón

In the past this was the palace of the Condestables de Castilla (the Constables of Castile). The Constable was the first officer of the crown and commander in chief of the military in the absence of the monarch. Today the palace is the head office of a bank, but its courtyard may be visited during working hours. Its name comes from the representation of a Franciscan cord which frames the main doorway. It is one of the finest examples of civil architecture in Burgos and it was here that the Catholic Monarchs received Columbus on his return from his first voyage to America.

El Castillo park

From this high point of the city you can see the ruins of the castle and parts of the old walls. From the surrounding park there are excellent views of a large part of the city and of the plain round about.

Arches

The Santa María arch is the most ornate, but if you also take the time to visit that of San Esteban and the gate to the

Pilgrims in a moment of uncertainty. Right: street in the old town.

Hospital del Rey, a one-time pilgrims' hospice, you may get an idea of what the old walls which surrounded the city must have looked like.

Plaza Mayor

This is a typical Castilian square, if a little irregular in shape, with arches on all sides. Together with the steep streets leading off to the north and west from the cathedral, it is the natural starting point for a walk through the old town.

Espolón and statue of El Cid

Beside the Espolón and the Teatro Principal you will find the equestrian statue of El Cid, who points towards the battlefield with his famous sword, Tizona. The Espolón itself is a pleasant tree-lined walk popular with the people of the city.

River Arlanzón

This is the river which runs around the south side of the city and separates the old town from the new. A stroll along its banks and over its bridges affords a view of the waterfowl swimming tranquilly in its waters.

The Condestables (the Constables)
Inside Burgos cathedral one of the places which most impresses the visitor is the chapel of the Condestables (see previous page). In the centre are the recumbent statues of the founders, Pedro Fernández de Velasco and Mencía de Mendoza. These marble statues are works of great realism, displaying exquisite detail in the representation of the features, hair, clothing and jewellery.

Las Huelgas monastery

This is one of the most important monuments of Burgos. Of particular note are its royal pantheon, cloister and, in the grounds, the Ricas Telas (rich fabrics) museum. Although outside the city, there are good bus links.

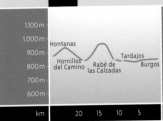

From Burgos to Hontanas
The valley of the Arlanzón

26.4 km • 7 h 10 min

Burgos – Villalbilla
1 h 20 min

While the stretch leading into Burgos is reviled, and rightly so, the route out of the city is pleasant. The transition from town to country takes place swiftly, without disagreeable industrial estates or blighted suburban landscapes between the two.

Start out up calle Fernán González, go round the back of the cathedral and, following inconspicuous but well-placed yellow arrows, come to the gate to the Hospital del Rey. Here you leave the old, walled quarters of the city behind.

Now go down the hill on which the old town stands and pass briefly through new neighbourhoods. You will come to the Malatos bridge, which takes you over the river Arlanzón. For the first half of the day you will be walking along its valley, encountering beautiful

The river Arlanzón near Tardajos

wooded areas by the banks and delighting in the riverside scenery.

Having crossed the river you come to the university campus area, with broad avenues where you need to pay attention to the yellow arrows, and then to a pleasant park. At present you are walking on the flat, but very shortly you will commence a gentle descent along a surfaced road to Villalbilla.

Right: a pilgrim entering Tardajos. Left: washing hung out to dry in the town.

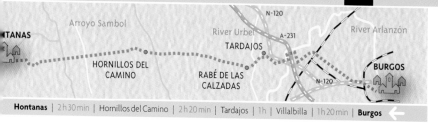

Hontanas | 2h30min | Hornillos del Camino | 2h20min | Tardajos | 1h | Villalbilla | 1h20min | **Burgos** ←

Villalbilla – Tardajos
2 h 20 min

You will see little of Villalbilla, as the Way goes round the outside of the town, although some pilgrims prefer to spend the night here to avoid the more crowded conditions of the hostels in Burgos. On leaving the town you take a rural track, which is flat and in very good condition.

Tardajos – Rabé de las Calzadas
2 h 55 min

Although on this stretch we encounter awkward infrastructures in the form of railway lines and main roads, you will get round them with little difficulty. You also pass underneath a motorway viaduct, which is a little intimidating. If you look closely you may see, on one of its concrete pillars, a small plaque apologizing for the detour that the building of the new road obliges the pilgrim to make. It is true that the road has caused just such a detour; however, on the positive side, the path now passes close to the river, which looks magnificent here, bordered by poplars, alders and some ashes.

Fountain with scallop shells in Rabé

You enter Tardajos passing beside the cross. This town has the best facilities of all those on the stage. There are bars and restaurants, grocery stores, a chemist's and a bank with an ATM. The other villages through which you will be passing are much smaller and their facilities are limited.

From Tardajos you take a local road to Rabé de las Calzadas. There is very little traffic and this is therefore an easy walk, although it is said that this was once an area of swamps so terrible that the local people used to offer up prayers for divine protection.

Rabé de las Calzadas – Fuente de Prao Torre
3 h 30 min

Rabé de las Calzadas, so called because it was the point where two Roman roads met, goes by in a flash, as it consists of little more than one long street where you will find a fountain with iron jets decorated with scallop shells.

From this village onwards, the landscape changes dramatically. You will now be walking across the broad, treeless plain of Castile, a lonely and monotonous landscape that can prove quite a tough psychological test for the traveller for several days. When you reach Tierra de Campos in Palencia after a couple of days the terrain will be uniformly flat as well, but today it is not only bare but also incorporates some steep inclines, as there are two hills to be crossed. Thus, on leaving Rabé you immediately face a sharp, 2 km ascent to Fuente de Prao.

The omnipresent vending machines
For the first two weeks of the pilgrimage you will find the Way full of vending machines. After that they become less common and finally disappear. It is not only drinks and snacks that they offer, however. Some also dispense first-aid material or even souvenir scallop shells. At some hostels, where breakfast is not served, they provide the only choice for the first meal of the day.

Fuente de Prao Torre – Hornillos del Camino
4 h 40 min

A picnic area, with tables, seats and bins, has been set up by this fountain. Taking a rest here is not a bad idea, as you have further to climb before reaching the top of the first hill. The track is broad but walking

Church and hostel (right) in Hornillos

is not easy, as there are deep ruts in the track left by the wheels of tractors and other agricultural machinery. What's more there are pebbles the size of tennis balls which will have twisted the ankle of more than one pilgrim. At around kilometre 14 of the stage you start to go steeply downward and follow that incline all the way to Hornillos del Camino.

Hornillos del Camino – Arroyo San Bol
6 h 5 min
Hornillos has facilities for the pilgrim and you may as well take advantage of them, as the stage is long and a couple of difficult stretches still lie ahead. The town has a pleasant corner in the little square of the church, where there is a fountain adorned with the figure of a cock.

On leaving Hornillos you at once face another climb as stiff as the last one. The descent to the stream called Arroyo San Bol begins as soon as you reach the top.

Arroyo San Bol – Hontanas
7 h 10 min
Some 200 m to the left of the Arroyo

Hontanas, half hidden in a hollow

San Bol there is a hostel which could provide the modern pilgrim with the closest equivalent to the former medieval experience. Almost everybody prefers, however, to continue to Hontanas, a town you come upon almost by surprise, as it lies in a hollow and is therefore not visible until you are practically on top of it.

Eating
Tardajos and Hornillos del Camino are the only towns along the stage where you can take a break at a bar or restaurant. However, while the facilities in Tardajos are reliable and there are also shops where you can stock up, in Hornillos the bar might be closed in the low season. In winter you may have similar problems in Hontanas and have some difficulty getting dinner. It is worth bearing these limitations in mind in the off-season.

Sleeping
There are three hostels in Hontanas. The municipal hostel (telephone 0034 947 377 021) is on calle Real near the entrance to the town. If it is full, additional facilities are available in the former schools. Both open all year round. There is also a privately-run hostel, El Puntido (telephone 0034 947 378 597), on calle de la Iglesia. As well as dormitories with bunk beds, it has some double rooms. It opens from Holy Week to October.

| km | 25 | 20 | 15 | 10 | 5 |

From Hontanas to Boadilla del Camino
Entering Palencia

28.5 km • 6 h 25 min

Hontanas – Convento de San Antón
1 h 10 min

On the previous stage you had to walk down into a hollow to get to Hontanas. It would seem only logical, therefore, that today you should expect to climb upward. Yet the stage begins with a gentle descent which takes you to the Convento de San Antón (monastery of Saint Anthony). For a little over an hour you have to walk along a road with no hard shoulder. There is not much traffic, but you will generally be covering this section early in the day when visibility may not be great. You should therefore be particularly careful and stick to the left-hand border.

Convento de San Antón – Castrojeriz
2h

The ruins of the monastery of Saint Anthony are one of the most

The arch of San Antón

pleasant surprises of the day on the architectural front. There is an enormous arch which once supported a roof, thus forming a porch which provided travellers with momentary shelter. Parts of the apse and of the façade of the church, together with some main walls of the central nave, are likewise still standing. You can also see the remains of the cupboards

Two aspects of the town of Castrojeriz, which the pilgrim crosses from end to end.

Pilgrim fighting against the wind at Alto de Mostelares

where the monks used to leave pilgrims a bite to eat.

The Order of Saint Anthony, which governed this monastery until it was dissolved at the end of the eighteenth century, was very powerful on the Way in its time. It was founded for the purpose of caring for those suffering from a disease very similar to leprosy, known as Saint Anthony's fire. The members of the community wore a habit bearing the Greek letter *tau* on the front. You will become very familiar with that letter, as you will see it repeatedly on T-shirts and other kinds of souvenir.

Note that the road passes directly under the Gothic arch. For some this is a clear sign that on this section the Way in its present form continues to follow the medieval route exactly. And, whether the exact medieval route or not, there are still four kilometres of tarmac to go on this stretch.

Castrojeriz – Alto de Mostelares
3 h

When you reach Castrojeriz it is a good idea, for various reasons, to call a brief halt. On the one hand, you have now been walking for a couple of hours. What's more, the town has a number of interesting monuments and it is worth having a rest and looking around. Furthermore, upon leaving you face a tough 10 km stretch with a high point of some significance before coming to the next town.

The citizens of Castrojeriz boast of having the longest urban crossing on the whole Way. Leaving the cities aside, that may perhaps be the case. However, of greater importance are the churches of Nuestra Señora de Manzano (Our Lady of the Apple Tree) and San Juan (Saint John), the imposing civil buildings and the Plaza Mayor, while the houses on calle Mayor are fine examples of Castilian architecture.

Alto de Mostelares – Fuente del Piojo
4h

On leaving Castrojeriz you come immediately to a broad, earth track. It is in good condition, but entirely exposed. Initially you may not feel the wind, as you are still heading down towards the river Odrilla.

From there you see that the path ahead climbs and veers to the right. The ascent looks intimidating and you will, indeed, gain over a hundred metres in height in little more than a kilometre. It is, in a way, a pleasant change to head for a point that will give you a broad horizon. However, when you actually reach the top, Alto de Mostelares, you may find the view a bit disheartening, as the endless plain stretches away to the town of Frómista and even beyond.

Alto de Mostelares has an enormous trig point on the right and a rest area on the left. Being exposed,

The start of a tough test
Although the last part of the preceding stage allowed you to form an idea of what lay ahead, it is on stage 14 that you come to the province of Palencia, where the Tierra de Campos puts the pilgrim to the harsh psychological trial of the plain. The horizon is flat and there are no visual references. For kilometres on end there are no towns, trees or even rocks that might serve as intermediate goals. Mental strength is required.

however, this is not the most comfortable place for a pause. It is better to go on to Fuente del Piojo, which will take about 45 minutes.

Fuente del Piojo – Ermita de San Nicolás
4 h 10 min

At Fuente del Piojo take advantage of the little picnic area installed there by the regional government of Castilla y León. You have now

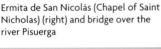

Ermita de San Nicolás (Chapel of Saint Nicholas) (right) and bridge over the river Pisuerga

Dawn in Boadilla and detail of the Roman mill at the entrance to the town the town

descended from Alto de Mostelares by its west side and what remains, from here to the end of the stage, is a fairly gentle section without inclines of any significance.

Ermita de San Nicolás – Itero de la Vega
4 h 40 min

Although in spring the ears of corn provide company of a sort, the landscape otherwise remains bare. Following the path you come to the Ermita de San Nicolás (Chapel of Saint Nicholas), a robust building lying to the left of the Way which was, in the golden age of the medieval pilgrimages, a noted hospice. It has been completely restored, but is closed. You are now very near to Fitero bridge, where you cross the Pisuerga and enter the province of Palencia. The river is generally quiet and calm, but the seven arches and humped back of the bridge speak of powerful swells in times of heavy rain.

Itero de la Vega – Boadilla del Camino
6 h 25 min

Between the village of Itero and the point of entry into Boadilla you will see just one tree. However, before finishing the stage you at least come to a climb and a little pine wood which break up the monotony of the landscape. Today you have had your first taste of Tierra de Campos.

Eating
On this stage there are bars, restaurants and shops to be found at Castrojeriz, Itero de la Vega and Boadilla del Camino. Have a break and take advantage of these facilities as the stage is long and demanding on both the physical and the psychological fronts.

Sleeping
There are three hostels in Boadilla del Camino. Albergue Putzu is the first you come to before entering the built-up area. It has no telephone, but contact can be made by email at inconformista@hotmail.com. It is open all year except at Christmas. Albergue de Boadilla del Camino, the municipal hostel (telephone 0034 979 810 390), is in the town centre and opens all year round. The third is called En el Camino (telephone 0034 979 810 284) and opens from March to early November. In general, pilgrims speak very favourably of all three and also remark on the friendliness of the people of the town.

Boadilla is the regular stage end for the many pilgrims who prefer not to go all the way to Frómista in a single day.

1.000 m
900 m — Carrión de los Condes
800 m — Boadilla del Camino
700 m — Villalcázar de Sirga · Frómista
600 m
500 m

km   15   10   5

From Boadilla del Camino to Carrión de los Condes
Tierra de Campos

21 km • 5 h 45 min

Boadilla del Camino – Frómista
1 h 20 min

The first five kilometres of this stage are easily the most beautiful in terms of landscape.

Leave Boadilla del Camino, still sheltered to some degree by the trees that are now so rare on the route, and at once you will realize that the terrain before you lies flat as far as the eye can see. Don't expect any significant changes of elevation or to see anything other than the immense fields of corn to either side of the Way. However, you soon come to a man-made feature which will make the rest of your walk to Frómista pleasant and interesting: the Canal de Castilla (Castile Canal). The purpose of this major work of engineering was to link the grain-growing lands of the plateau to the ports of Cantabria. Over 200 km of canals came into service, but

Beneath the summer sun at Villarmentero

unfortunately the goal of transporting the goods to the sea was never achieved. The walk along the towpath, beside elms, observing the birds in the reeds and hearing the slow movement of the water, goes all the way to Frómista, where a system of locks, crossed by a bridge, enabled boats to overcome the significant change of elevation at that point.

The church of San Martín (Saint Martin) in Frómista

Carrión | 1 h 15 min | Villalcázar | 1h 30 min | Revenga | 1h 40 min | Frómista | 1 h 20 min | **Boadilla**

Frómista – Campos

2 h 10 min

While the Canal de Castilla represents a brief but welcome variation in the uniformity of the landscape, the town of Frómista is one of the most attractive sights to be found along the Way in terms of religious architecture. The church of San Martín (Saint Martin), with its round towers flanking the main entrance, is a masterpiece of the Iberian Romanesque style. It stands apart in a rather graceless square, but this location at least means that you can admire the building from all four sides.

This church's exact name is San Martín de Tours (Saint Martin of Tours), and it is known to date back to the eleventh century, as it was mentioned in 1066. The restorations it underwent in the late nineteenth and early twentieth centuries have received as much criticism as its original structure has received praise. It has an octagonal cupola above the cross, while its cylindrical towers, acting as belfries, give it something of the appearance of a fortress. Inside there is a thirteenth-century figure of Christ. The naves are in general very sober, although on some of the columns there are capitals decorated with motifs that are biblical, such as the depiction of Adam and Eve, or relate to folk wisdom, like the fable of the fox and the grapes.

The church of San Martín is open

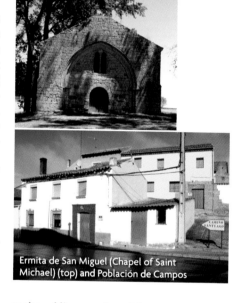

Ermita de San Miguel (Chapel of Saint Michael) (top) and Población de Campos

to the public every day of the year, mornings and afternoons, except 1 January and 25 December. Admission is one euro.

It is worthwhile taking a look at the rest of the town, especially since, this early in the stage, you will probably still have the energy to do so! The churches of San Pedro (Saint Peter) and Santa María del Castillo (Saint Mary of the Castle) can be visited and the fine adobe-built houses are good examples of this type of architecture. You will be coming across houses like these quite often during the rest of the day and on the stages which lie ahead.

A specimen of 'Way of Saint James art' in the town and pilgrims arriving at Villalcázar

Leaving Frómista you immediately come to a comfortable, well-kept earth track running to the right of the road. Flanked by an abundance of marker stones, it takes you in long, straight stretches, with a barely perceptible incline, to Población de Campos, which you will cross by way of the main street.

Campos – Revenga de Campos
3 h
At this stage you can take either the main route or a new one which has been opened up on the right. The new route is quieter, as it takes us away from the noise of the traffic, but also a little longer. A further point in its favour is that the last stretch, before Villarmentero, runs beside the river in an area with a few trees.

If you follow the main route, upon leaving Población de Campos cross the bridge over the river Ucieza and return to the earth track. Now there is nothing on the horizon to distract your attention. If you were hoping to make an introspective journey along the Way of Saint James you will find such landscape very conducive to this.

Did you bring binoculars?
As part of the rich experience of travelling the Way of Saint James you are in continuous contact not only with a magnificent historic heritage but also, evidently, with nature. Pilgrims who did not balk at the thought of carrying binoculars in their pack will frequently have the chance to observe the animal life, particularly the birds, more closely.

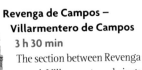

Revenga de Campos – Villarmentero de Campos
3 h 30 min
The section between Revenga and Villarmentero brings nothing new. The cornfields stretch away into the distance to left and right and there is nothing else to be seen.

Courtyard of the convent of Santa Clara
(Saint Clare) in Carrión de los Condes

Villarmentero de Campos – Villalcázar de Sirga

4 h 30 min

At Villarmentero the track starts to ascend a little. Before reaching Villalcázar de Sirga you will sense that you are coming to a steeper incline. Although the climb is not hard, it is quite long. If there is a wind, which is often the case in this area, you may find this stretch a little difficult.

Villalcázar de Sirga – Carrión de los Condes

5 h 45 min

After Villalcázar de Sirga the incline becomes sharper and the noise of the vehicles louder, as those heading downhill tend to move at high speed.

On entering Carrión de los Condes you at once come to the convent of Santa Clara (Saint Clare) with its beautiful courtyard. There is no need to hurry to find accommodation. Why not take a walk around the centre and consider the options before making a choice. Sometimes an ordinary-looking building proves to be more inviting than a historic one.

Eating

With the exception of Villarmentero, all the towns on this stage have bars and/or restaurants. Revenga de Campos and Villalcázar, which are intermediate points, also have shops. Pausing from time to time is highly recommended, given that this stage, although not very long and without difficult inclines, is psychologically wearing. Furthermore, if the wind is blowing the traveller will also feel physically tired at the end of the day.

Sleeping

In Carrión de los Condes there is plenty of choice. On the one hand, there are three hostels. The Espíritu Santo (telephone 0034 979 880 052) is run by nuns and the treatment is maternal. It opens all year. The parish hostel, Santa María (telephone 0034 979 880 768), is similarly run by nuns and opens from March to October.

The third is the convent of Santa Clara (telephone 0034 979 880 837), which stands by the entrance to the town. Although the building is certainly noteworthy, this hostel is without doubt the most basic of the three in terms of amenities and receives the lowest rating from pilgrims. It opens from March to November. The town also has a youth hostel, various guest or boarding houses and a luxury hotel.

1.000 m
900 m — Lédigos Calzadilla de la Cueza
800 m — Terradillos de los Templarios Carrión de los Condes
700 m
600 m
500 m

km   20   15   10   5

From Carrión de los Condes to Terradillos
A straight line on a bare plain

22.4 km • 5 h 55 min

Carrión de los Condes – Abadía de Benevívere
1 h 5 min

At present Carrión de los Condes does not have even a fifth of the population it had in the Middle Ages, when it was one of the pillars of the Way of Saint James in Castile. Its heritage is immense, however, and it is worth having a look around the town before starting the long stretch across the lonely plain.

The first monument you come to, upon entering the town, is the convent of Santa Clara. It has an excellent courtyard and a museum housing some valuable works of art. It is one of the oldest Order of Saint Clare convents in Spain, dating from the mid-thirteenth century. The cakes made by the nuns who live there have become quite famous.

In the centre of the town you come to two imposing churches. Santa María del Camino (Saint

Monument to the pilgrim in Carrión de los Condes

Mary of the Way) is Romanesque and dates from the eleventh century. Its south façade is porticoed and displays a representation of the tribute of the hundred maidens which the Christians were obliged to make to the Moors during the time of Muslim rule. It was precisely as a consequence of that tribute that in the year 844 the Christians fought the battle of Clavijo where, thanks to the miraculous intervention of Saint James on a white horse, they defeated the Moors. Inside the church there is a thirteenth-century figure of the Virgen del Camino (Our Lady of the Way).

Further along the calle Mayor you find the church of Santiago (Saint James). This twelfth-century Romanesque church is one of the most important of its style in all Spain. You will notice the richness of the frieze of the façade, depicting a seated Christ Pantocrator surrounded by the apostles and elders. Inside there is a museum of religious art which has

A sign indicating the halfway point of the Way and the hostel at Calzadilla de la Cueza

various valuable pieces of different styles, including a fifteenth-century figure of the Piedad (Our Lady of Pity) and various figures of Christ crucified.

Continuing up the street, you come to the door of the surprising Teatro Sarabia, a fine example of nineteenth-century architecture of its kind with a very well-kept interior. It has a regular programme of plays and performances and forms part of the network of historic theatres of Castilla y León.

There are many other buildings of architectural, artistic and historic value in Carrión, including the ancestral houses in the old town, but it is time to get going. Arrows and signs, indicating that Santiago lies 400 km ahead, guide you up a gentle slope and out of the centre. Cross the bridge over the river

Carrión and you come to the monastery of San Zoilo (Saint Zoilo), a building on an impressive scale dating from the mid-eleventh century. It belonged, over time, to various religious orders. Now most of the rooms have been restored and made into a luxury hotel. Although this is modern, its

Carrión de los Condes

Mirages

To call this part of the plain of Palencia a desert would be excessive. However, on stage 16 the straight stretch of over 17 km running from Carrión de los Condes to Calzadilla de la Cueza sometimes holds a surprise in store. Because of the intense heat and the refraction of light rays, objects ahead may seem to be floating on a liquid surface. This is an optical phenomenon which lasts only some seconds.

architects have endeavoured to respect most of the original elements of historic value. Nearby you may see some large marker stones displaying coats of arms of certain historic communities.

You now continue along a tarmacked road, although there is hardly any traffic. The land is entirely flat. You walk for about an hour before coming to the old abbey of Benevívere, founded in 1065. These days it is enclosed within private grounds, but it seems, from what you can see through the fence, that some barely recognizable remains are all that is left of the historic building.

Abadía de Benevívere – Calzadilla de la Cueza

3 h 45 min

Some 800 m on from the ruins of the old abbey you come to a rather uncomfortable, stony path. This is the Cañada Real Leonesa and, at the same time, the original Way. You will come across some boulders on which information of interest to pilgrims has been carved. The Romans once trod these same stones, as this was, originally, part of the road they called Via Aquitania, which ran between Astorga and Bordeaux.

There are occasional trees and streams, but in general the

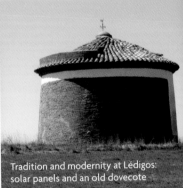

Tradition and modernity at Lédigos: solar panels and an old dovecote

Notice at a hostel and adobe architecture at Terradillos de Templarios

landscape is flat, monotonous and even hypnotic, given the absence of visual references on which to focus.

Three hours will go by before you see the tower of the cemetery of Calzadilla in the distance. It will then take almost another hour to reach that town.

Calzadilla de la Cueza – Lédigos
5 h 10 min

Pilgrims who have reached this point may subsequently find that the rest of the Way seems to fly by, as they will have come through the toughest psychological test that the pilgrimage poses. The names of the streets in Calzadilla are a curious feature of the town: Travesía Mayor I, II, III. At least it is a very simple system. On leaving Calzadilla you take a very good track which leads to Lédigos.

Lédigos – Terradillos de Templarios
5 h 55 min

The church at Lédigos has three images of Saint James: as apostle, as pilgrim and as Moor-slayer. As it is generally closed, you have to ask for it to be opened. From Lédigos to Terradillos de Templarios you will not take the road but, instead, the optional route running at a higher level beside the fields. It is clearly marked.

Eating
Calzadilla de la Cueza and Lédigos, the two intermediate points on the stage, have bars and/or restaurants. However, only the latter, which is reached towards the end of the stage, has a shop. It is necessary to bear this in mind and therefore to carry sufficient supplies and, above all, water.

Sleeping
Terradillos de Templarios is an example of the impact of the Way of Saint James on local economies. It has two hostels which, together, can accommodate over a hundred people.

The Jacques de Molay (telephone 0034 979 883 679) has rooms for three and six persons. Los Templarios (telephone 0034 667 252 279) even has single and double rooms. Both sell basic supplies and serve dinners and breakfasts, as there are no other facilities in the town.

1,000 m
900 m
800 m
700 m
600 m
500 m

El Burgo Ranero · Bercianos del Real Camino · Terradillos de Templarios · Sahagún

km 25 20 15 10 5

From Terradillos to El Burgo Ranero
Coming into León

26.8 km • 7 h

Terradillos de Templarios – Moratinos
45 min

There are two options at the start of this stage: continue along the track running beside the road or, instead, go for the alternative route via Moratinos and San Nicolás del Real Camino. The latter is better: it takes you away from the noise and the traffic, is more 'pastoral' and does not make the total distance any greater.

The alternative route follows a broad, level track between cornfields. The going is easy and you reach Moratinos in just three quarters of an hour. The village, which is crossed in no time, stands on the edge of a dip and the locals say that this position makes it cooler than the majority of towns on the plain.

A gentle slope leads upward out of Moratinos, the last town of Palencia.

Pilgrims at Ermita Virgen del Puente (Chapel of Our Lady of the Bridge)

Moratinos – San Nicolás del Real Camino
1 h 20 min

San Nicolás del Real Camino was an important point on the Way in medieval times. It was the site of a hospital founded at the end of the twelfth century where lepers were given refuge. Nothing remains of the building now. There is a bar in the village where you might want to take a break, as there are no more facilities until you reach Sahagún.

First view of Moratinos. On the right, traditional constructions in the hillside

El Burgo Ranero | 1 h 45 min | Bercianos | 2 h 20 min | Sahagún | 1 h 35 min | San Nicolás | 1 h 20 min | **Terradillos de Templarios**

San Nicolás del Real Camino – Ermita Virgen del Puente
2 h 30 min

You cross the river Sequillo and at once come to a well-looked-after rural track. The only things to see here are the small birds perched on the posts and branches. The landscape affords little variety, although there are clusters of trees from time to time. Just before coming to the river Valveraduey turn to the right and rejoin the main route coming from Terradillos de Templarios. There is no risk of making a mistake, as the yellow arrows are large and frequent. Walk for about a hundred metres to the right of the road and then veer further to the right along a pathway which leads to the beautiful stone bridge over the river and so to the chapel called, appropriately, Virgen del Puente (Our Lady of the Bridge).

The chapel is closed and although you can peer though a little window it is difficult to see anything inside. It has, however, been well restored outside. There is a picnic area with tables and benches and an 'artistic' arrangement of rusting metal seats propped against the walls. Sahagún can be seen from here. However, although the route offered by the preferred pathway is pleasant, it is also rather roundabout, whereas if you return to the road you will advance in a straight line.

Cyclist at the hostel in Sahagún

Ermita Virgen del Puente – Sahagún
2 h 55 min

You have left the province of Palencia behind and are now in that of León. You will be crossing it from east to west at one of its broadest points. This section will take you a week.

About half an hour after having left the chapel, we come to Sahagún. Here the route can prove a little difficult to follow, because although the yellow arrows lead to the centre of the town they then tend to disappear.

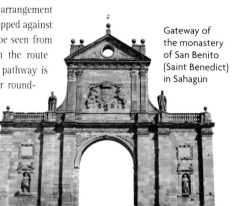

Gateway of the monastery of San Benito (Saint Benedict) in Sahagún

Volunteer *hospitaleros*
Many of the *hospitaleros* who assist at the hostels on the Way are volunteers. They are people with a firm belief in solidarity who receive no payment for what they do and even have to pay some of their own travelling expenses. They nearly always stand out for their good humour and friendliness, qualities which are at times lacking in some of the paid employees.

Sahagún – Calzada del Coto junction

4 h

Sahagún is one of the towns which prospered greatly under the powerful order of Cluny, which at one time controlled as many as 300 monasteries and churches along the Way. Numerous buildings survive to remind pilgrims of the splendour of that period. Two obvious examples are the churches of San Tirso (Saint Thyrsus) and San Lorenzo (Saint Lawrence), with their great bell towers full of windows. These will appeal particularly to lovers of the Mudejar style.

Another noteworthy building is the Benedictine monastery, which dated from the beginning of the twelfth century. Unfortunately, all that remains of it today is the chapel of San Mancio (Saint Mancio), the tower and the arch of San Benito. This archway may look a little odd since it stands alone and an avenue, carrying traffic, passes beneath it. However, it was once the south entrance to the church of the monastery.

Also worth a visit are the Torre del Reloj (clock tower) and the pilgrims' hostel, located in the building of the former church of la Trinidad (the Trinity).

You leave Sahagún passing beside the church of San Lorenzo. The arrows disappear in calle Antonio Nicolás, but just follow the natural downward inclination of the streets. You will see a monument to the pilgrim consisting of a staff and the prints of boots in rusted iron beside a rock with a plaque. From that point on the yellow arrows reappear and lead to Canto bridge over the river Cea. Follow the rather boring track until you come to Calzada de Coto junction, where the

Chapel of Nuestra Señora de Perales (Our Lady of the Pear Trees) near Bercianos

The lake of Burgo Ranero. Left: Local people in the shade

route divides. From here an alternative path follows the course of the old Roman road to Mansilla de las Mulas. Continue beside the road, passing close to a wayside cross.

Calzada del Coto junction – Ermita Nuestra Señora de Perales
4 h 45 min

On this stretch there is no traffic. Walk along close to the tarmac until you come to the pretty chapel of Perales.

Ermita Nuestra Señora de Perales – Bercianos del Real Camino
5 h 15 min

The chapel is an ideal place for a picnic or a rest. Bercianos is close by. There are a few trees, but otherwise the landscape is bare.

Bercianos del Real Camino – El Burgo Ranero
7 h

After a walk of almost two hours on the plain, you come to the pleasantly surprising town of El Burgo Ranero.

Eating

Sahagún is strategically located three hours from your starting point. It is a large place where you will find bars, restaurants and grocery shops. Between there and the end of the stage the only other place with similar facilities is Bercianos. So do make sure that you have enough water for this section.

Sleeping

Thanks to another apparent 'miracle' worked by the demands of the Way of Saint James, El Burgo Ranero has various hostels. The Domenico Laffi (telephone 0034 987 330 047) is conveniently positioned at one end of the main street. It opens all year and operates on voluntary donations. El Nogal (telephone 0034 627 229 331) stands at the entrance to the town and is privately run. La Laguna (telephone 0034 987 330 094) is at the opposite end. Both open from Holy Week to November. The Ebalo Tamaú (telephone 0034 679 490 521) is at calle La Estación, 37. It opens from early April to mid-October. There are also a couple of boarding houses in the town. The albergue de Calzadilla de los Hermanillos (Tel. 0034 987 330 023) is in the nearby town of the same name.

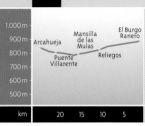

From El Burgo Ranero to Arcahueja
An infinite path

25.1 km • 6 h 40 min

El Burgo Ranero – Reliegos
2 h 55 min

In these near-desert surroundings, El Burgo Ranero might at first glance look like a typical small town where you can rest and remove your boots, but with nothing else to recommend it. However, you need only take a short walk and have a careful look around in order to see that this is a town that offers a great deal.

The hostel (Domenico Laffi) is the first surprise. It stands at one end of the calle Mayor (formerly called calle del Camino Francés, a name which shows the importance that the pilgrimage has always had for this town) and is built using a traditional method which mixes clay and straw bricks. The resulting warm brown colour blends fully into the landscape. Inside there is a fireplace by which you can sit and talk in the evening, and as the rooms upstairs have no ceiling there is an interesting view of the wood and vegetable fibre structure which forms the basis of the roof.

This form of construction is by no means a rarity in El Burgo Ranero. rather the opposite. Walking through the town you will see many buildings of this type which have survived the passage of time. First and most important among them is the church, crowned with a weathercock, which looks magnificent in the golden evening light. It is usually closed, but if you ask around in the vicinity you can generally find someone with a key. Inside there is a sixteenth-century,

A traditional wine cellar, built into the hillside, in Reliegos

Detail of a window in the town and porticoed square in Mansilla de las Mulas

Renaissance, multicoloured wood altarpiece. There also used to be a valuable figure of the Virgen de las Nieves or Virgen Manca (Our Lady of the Snows) but this is now in the museum of León cathedral.

The locals like a chat and will tell you all about the birds you might see on the nearby lake. This lies just to the west of the town. Bounded by reeds and of a fair size, it is frequented by small birds and visited by a range of waterfowl throughout the year.

Following this leisurely stroll through El Burgo Ranero, brace yourself for what is the second-longest stretch of the Way without a town or village. You will spend almost three hours on a plain where the only variation is an insignificant change in altitude. The track is in good condition and although it runs beside a road there is very little traffic. There are cornfields to either side. About an hour after starting out you come to a picnic and rest area. Although you may not feel tired as yet, bear in mind that there are still eight kilometres to Reliegos.

Reliegos – Mansilla de las Mulas
4 h 15 min

Just before coming to Reliegos you take the underpass beneath the railway line, following the yellow arrows. You then come to the first houses.

Although the locals say that vine growing has practically died out in the town, your attention will be drawn to the town's curious old wine cellars. Some of these were visible in the distance on the previous stage, but now you have a chance to take a closer look. They are cut into the low hillsides, thus ensuring constant humidity, temperature and darkness. On the outside they may have a façade or, sometimes, not even that: just a door. It is true, however, that they no longer serve their original purpose. Now they are used as warehouses or, more commonly, for family reunions and the like.

It was at Reliegos that the original Astorga–Bordeaux Roman road and the French Way crossed. Those keen on history should make a point of visiting the church, dedicated to San Cornelio (Saint Cornelius) (pope) and San Cipriano (Saint Cyprian) (bishop), while those who are interested in measurements may be interested in the local refrain 'the well-measured league lies between Reliegos and Mansilla'. Having heard this, it would not be a surprise to discover that some good-humoured soul had put up a rudimentary wooden sign to inform pilgrims that they were precisely one league away from Mansilla de las Mulas.

Mansilla de las Mulas – Villamoros de Mansilla
5 h 20 min
From the moment you leave Reliegos the outline of Mansilla

The blessing of the walkways
On the vast plains of northern Castile the pilgrim may often have the sensation of walking on a conveyor belt which is moving in the opposition direction. The psychological hardship of this part of the Way is, however, greatly mitigated by the existence of walkways: earth tracks opened up parallel to roads which save the traveller dozens of hours of dangerous proximity to traffic. They are a blessing.

may be seen. This is encouraging, even though you know full well that there is a league to cover. The walkway remains as monotonous as before.

You enter Mansilla de las Mulas through one of the surviving gates of its old wall of adobe and boulders, which dates from the twelfth century. You must cross the whole town, as the route leaves by the opposite end. This gives you the opportunity to admire its beautiful centre, with porticoed squares in the traditional style of Castile and León.

The stretch between Mansilla de las Mulas and Villamoros de Mansilla is the worst on the stage, as you have to walk beside a noisy, dusty road in somewhat suburban surroundings.

The river Porma at Puente de Villarente

Three shots of the tranquil town of Arcahueja

Villamoros de Mansilla – Puente de Villarente
5 h 40 min

Crossing Villamoros is unpleasant, as the walkway disappears for the duration and you have to walk along the hard shoulder of the road, which is uncomfortably narrow (when it is there at all). Fortunately, this stretch is short.

Puente de Villarente – Arcahueja
6 h 40 min

After crossing the unusual curved bridge over the river Porma, you pass through Puente de Villarente and then take an unattractive track running beneath pylons to the town of Arcahueja.

Eating

Stage 18 is a testing one. It tends to be very long, although in this guide we have preferred to stop at a rather unusual point precisely so that the distance is not too much. The towns along the stage are far apart, although all of them, with the exception of Villamoros de Mansilla, at least have a bar, restaurant and grocery store. It is necessary, however, to carry sufficient water, above all for the first section, which entails a walk of over three hours with nothing other than cornfields on either side of the path.

Sleeping

If you were to go on to the city of León, at a distance of 8 km, this stage would become rather arduous. For this reason this section stops at Arcahueja. Bear in mind, however, that the town has only one hostel, La Torre (telephone 0034 669 660 914), which has just ten beds. In the high season it will fill up very quickly. The hostel is open all year except at Christmas and in February. Dinner and breakfast are served and private rooms are also available. Arcahueja also has a hotel, which stands beside the road.

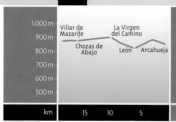

From Arcahueja to Villar de Mazarife
Surprising churches

| km | 15 | 10 | 5 | 24.9 km • 6 h 40 min |

Arcahueja – Valdelafuente
20 min

Leave Arcahueja on the side opposite the N-120 road. The route is well marked. Coming out of the town take a broad earth track leading upward through industrial surroundings and very soon you come to Valdelafuente.

Valdelafuente – Alto del Portillo
45 min

If you have no need to go into Valdelafuente follow the arrows which take you upward to Alto del Portillo, a mountain pass now disfigured by an enormous traffic roundabout and industrial estates. Some pilgrims have tried to make the place look a bit more human by attaching little wooden crosses to the wire fence, but it remains, even so, rather forbidding. Under no circumstances attempt to cross the main road at this point. It has

The church of the Virgen del Camino

multiple lanes and a concrete barrier in the middle and is very dangerous.

Alto del Portillo – León
2 h

The arrows, which are a little far apart here, lead you next to an industrial estate and subsequently into a small development. If you see a group of television and telephone masts ahead you'll know that you are on the right path. Before reaching them though, you will see a well-marked turn which takes you sharply downward through a pine wood and then by open fields. Here the arrows disappear, but you only need continue along the main track leading

Rest area at the Villar junction

Villar de Mazarife | 1h | Chozas de Abajo | 2 h 5 min | La Virgen del Camino | 1 h 35 min | León | 2 h | **Arcahueja**

towards the blocks of flats on the horizon. To the right you can now make out the spires of the cathedral of León. This is further confirmation that you are going in the right direction. You cross a bridge over the main road and so come safely to the town of Puente del Castro. Moving on, you see a fountain and arrows, in ever greater number, leading you along a pleasant urban walk into the old town of León.

León – Trobajo del Camino
2 h 40 min

If you have made an early start and it has only taken two hours to reach the doors of León cathedral, find a bar or a hostel where you can leave your backpack and take a leisurely look around the city (see pages 114–117). After the visit, your route out of the city takes you past the historic basilica of San Isidoro (Saint Isidore) and monastery of San Marcos (Saint Mark) and then over the river Bernesga.

This stretch is almost entirely urban, running between suburbs all the way to Trobajo.

Trobajo del Camino – La Virgen del Camino
3 h 40 min

You continue walking on tarmac, in an urban and somewhat industrial

Unusual bell tower at Chozas de Abajo

environment, for the space of the hour that separates Trobajo from La Virgen del Camino. But while you were previously walking on level ground, you are now faced with a more testing uphill stretch. However, you reach the high point of the stage shortly before coming to La Virgen del Camino and what remains ahead poses little difficulty.

Disgraceful competition

On leaving La Virgen del Camino you can either walk to the left of the N-120 road, through tranquil, rural surroundings, or take the walkway, which is more direct but noisy and less pleasant, to Villadangos del Páramo. We recommend the first of these routes, but the choice is, of course, up to you. However, just at the junction you will find numerous signs painted on the road inviting the pilgrim to take one route or the other. These have apparently been placed there by the owners of local businesses, who are, furthermore, also in the habit of crossing out those of their competitors. Near Oncina, Valverde and San Miguel it gets worse, because the arrows painted there only lead to the door of some bar, with no connection to the Way, and so cause the unwary traveller to walk additional kilometres for no reason whatsoever. At no other point on the Way is this disgraceful fight for business, which should certainly be stopped, so intense.

La Virgen del Camino – Fresno del Camino

4 h 5 min

The main attraction of La Virgen del Camino is without doubt the sanctuary, built in the 1960s. Those familiar with the work of the sculptor Josep María Subirachs will at once see that the bronze figures adorning the façade are his. On leaving the town you cross the road, go down a well-marked incline and pass by the stretch with the painted signs (see box above). The route to Fresno is

Route through the old town in León

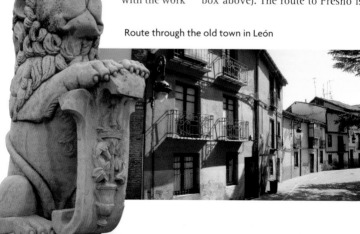

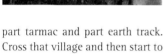

Monument to the pilgrim in Villar de Mazarife and church bell tower

part tarmac and part earth track. Cross that village and then start to go uphill.

Fresno del Camino – Oncina de Valdeoncina
4 h 30 min

The plain of León is not so psychologically tough as that of Palencia. Although the terrain is barren, there are inclines and some trees to liven up the path. Onward to Oncina.

Oncina de Valdeoncina – Chozas de Abajo
5 h 40 min

Passing by some of the oaks which are occasionally to be found on this plain, you come to the town of Chozas de Abajo with its peculiar iron bell tower (see page 111).

Chozas de Abajo – Villar de Mazarife
6 h 40 min

A straight, level stretch, which becomes rather tiring towards the end, takes you to Villar de Mazarife and the end of the day's stage.

Eating
From the standpoint of facilities this is one of the simplest stages. You reach León shortly after starting out and can buy supplies there or, if you prefer, have lunch after looking around the city. Alternatively there are bars or restaurants in La Virgen del Camino, Valverde de la Virgen or San Miguel del Camino.

There are also shops in La Virgen del Camino before starting on the preferred route towards Villar de Mazarife.

Sleeping
There are three hostels in Villar de Mazarife.

San Antonio de Padua (telephone 0034 987 390 192) opens all year and serves dinner and breakfast. Casa de Jesús (telephone 0034 987 390 697) likewise opens all year but only has vending machines. Tio Pepe (telephone 0034 987 390 517) usually opens from March to December.

León
A universe of coloured glass

Cathedral

According to the experts, León cathedral is the purest Gothic-style building in Spain. Work on its construction, over the Romanesque church that previously occupied the site, began in 1205. Its architects drew their inspiration from Rheims cathedral, although that of León is smaller.

It has five portals. The one which arouses the greatest admiration is that of the Last Judgement, so called because of the scene carved in stone in the tympanum. There is also an image of Nuestra Señora de las Nieves (Our Lady of the Snows).

The most remarkable elements of the interior are the stained glass (see box on page 117), the retrochoir, the choir with its fifteenth-century carved walnut stalls, and the main altar. Also noteworthy are the cloister and the various chapels.

Plaza Mayor and Barrio Húmedo

The old town of León is known as the Barrio Húmedo ('the wet quarter'). It is noted for its traditional architecture, its somewhat labyrinthine layout and, particularly, for its lively atmosphere, as this is the area favoured by the local people for drinks and tapas. The Plaza Mayor, dominated by the old city hall, is magnificent.

Main façade of the cathedral and (right) calle Ancha

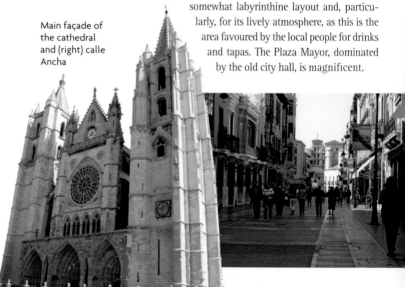

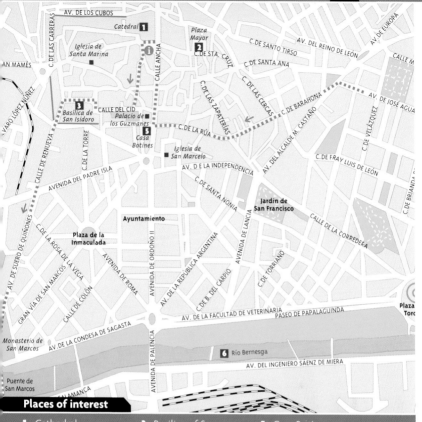

Places of interest

1 Cathedral
2 Plaza Mayor and
   Barrio Húmedo
3 Basilica of San
   Isidoro
4 Monastery of San
   Marcos
5 Casa Botines
6 River Bernesga
7 MUSAC

Eating
The dishes of León tend to be hearty. As the winters are so cold, stews and broths have always been popular. Sausages and cured beef also feature prominently. The centre of León is full of restaurants of all kinds. Among the most noted are El Cercao at calle La Bodega, 4 (telephone 0034 987 280 128), Bodega Regla at calle Regidores, 9–11 (telephone 0034 987 213 173) and Palacio Jabalquinto at calle Juan de Arfe, 2 (telephone 0034 987 215 322).

Sleeping
There are two hostels in León. The one nearest the centre is that of the Benedictine nuns (telephone 0034 987 252 866). It is open all year, but closes for the night at a very early hour. The other is the Ciudad de León (telephone 0034 987 081 832) which is municipal. It likewise opens all year and does not close its doors at night. It is, however, further away from the Barrio Húmedo. There is, in addition, a broad range of accommodation of other kinds. In the old town you can find various interesting choices. To mention just a few, there is Pensión Blanca B&B at calle Villafranca, 2 (telephone 0034 987 251 991), Pensión La Torre at calle La Torre, 3 (telephone 0034 987 225 594) and Pensión Sandoval at calle Hospicio, 19 (telephone 0034 987 212 041).

Basilica of San Isidoro (Saint Isidore)

The Way takes us directly in front of the basilica, which stands very near the cathedral and is considered one of Spain's most valuable Romanesque buildings. It dates from the tenth century and takes its name from the saint buried inside, although it is in fact dedicated to Saint John the Baptist. Its frescos are so outstanding that it has been called 'the Sistine Chapel of the Romanesque'. The main chapel has an altarpiece comprising twenty-four Renaissance panels.

Modern sculpture dedicated to the family in the centre of León

Monastery of San Marcos (Saint Mark)

The Way likewise leads us past the old monastery of San Marcos. This was a pilgrims' hospice until well into the twelfth century, subsequently becoming the seat of the order of Saint James. It is now a *parador* (state-run luxury hotel) but one can at least look around its main foyer. Its enormous plateresque façade of over a hundred metres in length commands a great esplanade close to the river Bernesga. Over the main portal we see a representation of Saint James the Moor-slayer mounted on his horse.

Casa Botines

The original owners of the fabrics warehouse which stood here were Catalans by the name of Botinàs. Their successors

A sunny morning in León's Plaza Mayor

Details of the cathedral doorway

portal. Inside, the upper floors are naturally illuminated by the skylights so characteristic of Gaudí's buildings. Now the building is the head office of a bank and, unfortunately, the interior is closed to visitors.

River Bernesga

The Bernesga runs all along the west side of the city. The river banks have been developed for the benefit of the citizens who can thus enjoy a pleasant stroll along the riverside and over the bridges. Some bars, restaurants and cultural centres have also sprung up and this has, as a result, become one of the favourite leisure areas of the city.

MUSAC

From the moment that the Museum of Contemporary Art (MUSAC) was opened, the flow of tourism towards León registered a spectacular increase. Other cities have witnessed that same effect upon becoming host to cultural institutions of similar importance. The museum's colourful façade constitutes a tribute to the famous stained glass of the cathedral.

Prodigious stained-glass windows
One of the cathedral's greatest treasures is its stained glass. It has three rose windows, thirty-one windows each twelve metres in height and other pieces, yielding a total stained-glass surface of 1,800 square metres. Biblical scenes are depicted. On sunny days the stained-glass fills the interior with light like a kaleidoscope. On festivals the windows are lit up from midnight to two in the morning, creating a spectacle worthy of admiration from the outside.

1.000 m
900 m
800 m
700 m
600 m
500 m

Astorga
San Justo de la Vega
Santibáñez de Valdeiglesias
Villar de Mazarife
Villavante
Puente y Hospital de Órbigo

km   20   15   10   5

From Villar de Mazarife to Astorga
Crossing the Órbigo without a fight

26.5 km • 7 h 5 min

Villar de Mazarife – Villavante
2 h 5 min

From Villar de Mazarife there are only 25 kilometres of the monotonous plain of Castilla y León still remaining. To know this may come as a relief, but you should also be warned that on the first hours of this section you will be walking on absolutely flat terrain without any landmarks.

For the first hour you walk on tarmac, along a local road with an almost eerie absence of vehicles. Subsequently, on reaching Milla del Páramo, you take a broad, stony track where progress is easier. Here we once again encounter the misleading signs, painted by rival businesses, of the kind described on page 112. Ignore the arrows that point to the right and instead carry on along the broad track until you come, an hour later, to Villavante.

Crucero de San Toribio

Villavante – Puente y Hospital de Órbigo
3 h 5 min

Walk through the streets of Villavante, following the signs which are very clear, passing by the church and beside a series of traditional adobe houses whose doors and frames are painted the classic blue to repel insects. You leave by way of a well-marked track similar to the one which led you to the town. Walk for some 300 m beside the railway line and then take a bridge over the motorway. Shortly before reaching the bridge over the river Órbigo you are walking on tarmac once again, remaining on it until you reach the cobblestones of the medieval bridge, which has its own beautiful story to tell.

The church at Villavante, with a balcony beneath the bell gable

The incredible bridge over the river Órbigo

Puente y Hospital de Órbigo – Villares de Órbigo
3 h 45 min

Pause for a while, take off your backpack and enjoy the sight of the magnificent bridge over the river Órbigo. It is the longest on the Way, having no fewer than nineteen arches and making more than one change of direction along its length. The murmur of running water, the birdsong and the sound of the breeze in the poplars along the banks are particularly relaxing. However, before crossing look carefully in case a knight in armour is barring your passage.

The story goes that in the year 1434, in accordance with a promise he had given to a lady, Suero de Quiñones mounted guard on the bridge from 10 July to 10 August and challenged whoever might wish to cross to a joust. The episode came to be called *El Paso Honroso* (the Honourable Pass). He found himself with plenty to do, as it is said that in that space of time 166 opponents faced him. He defeated them all.

Having crossed the bridge, without a fight, you come to the town of Puente y Hospital de Órbigo, a pleasant place with many facilities for the pilgrim.

Villares de Órbigo – Santibáñez de Valdeiglesias
4 h 20 min

On leaving Puente y Hospital de Órbigo you come to a fork marked with a large sign. There are two

Improvised monument on the Way

possible routes. If you go left you will progress in more or less a straight line along an easy walkway which, however, runs close beside the main N-120 road. A better option is to go right, where you will find a broad, level path, with some loose pebbles, which also takes you to Astorga. It is only a little longer, the landscape is more attractive and, above all, you do not have to hear the traffic. Keeping an eye out for the irrigation channels and ditches which appear from time to time beside the path, you soon come to Villares de Órbigo.

The signs you see on leaving Villares can be a little confusing. If you take the local road which turns to the left you will shortly find yourself on the very walkway you previously chose not to take. Instead cross the road and continue up a fairly steep little hill. You then come gently down on the other side towards Santibáñez de Valdeiglesias.

Santibáñez de Valdeiglesias – Crucero de San Toribio
5 h 55 min

You will at once notice that the landscape is changing. The plain is

Stocking up on energy

The city of Astorga is famous for its confectionery. In the centre there are many shops which sell the local specialities and at weekends fill with tourists eager to take home something sweet. These products have plenty of calories, occupy relatively little space and may prove useful to the pilgrim in moments of fatigue. It is quite a good idea to put a few in your backpack for later.

now behind you and, from Santibáñez de Valdeiglesias onwards, you will encounter a series of climbs. The terrain is not demanding, however, and is certainly more interesting. In addition, small oak woods, together with some holm oaks and box trees, begin to dot the

The episcopal palace in Astorga, designed by the architect Antoni Gaudí

landscape. On leaving Santibáñez de Valdeiglesias you will find, in a wood, an anonymous monument in the form of a dummy dressed in the traditional style. There are also some 'altars' with votive offerings left by travellers. However, they are not particularly attractive and do nothing at all to improve on what nature has already provided.

Detail of the façade of Astorga cathedral

You then come to one of the notable features of the day, the Crucero de San Toribio (Cross of Saint Turibius). From here you can see, on the plain below, the two towns which still lie ahead.

Crucero de San Toribio – San Justo de la Vega
6 h 10 min

A rather steep slope leads downhill from the cross. A cement path has been laid, however, so that the local people can walk here without having to tread in mud. The path is not in the best condition in places, but it is easy to walk on to San Justo de la Vega. You have to cross this town and the river Tuerto.

San Justo de la Vega – Astorga
7 h 5 min

It takes less than an hour to reach Astorga. The terrain is completely flat and you follow a very pleasant path, between poplars, away to the right of the road, with no industrial estate in sight.

Take the level crossing over the railway line and so come to the slope taking you up into Astorga, where you have four hostels to choose from.

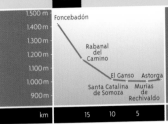

From Astorga to Foncebadón
Towards the Montes de León

20.9 km • 5 h 35 min

Astorga – Murias de Rechivaldo
50 min

Before setting out, allow yourself a little time to look round Astorga. The most important feature of the old town is the Plaza Mayor, where the magnificent town hall stands. The façade of the building dates from 1675 and the famous Maragatos clock from the eighteenth century. The square is typically

Restored house in Murias de Rechivaldo

porticoed and houses numerous bars and cafés which the locals frequent, particularly at weekends and on holidays. There is also an interesting old-fashioned pharmacy with jars of traditional potions.

The city's most outstanding monuments are the episcopal palace and the cathedral, which are practically side by side.

The bishop's residence is the work

Ecce Homo chapel at Valdeviejas

of the Catalan architect Antoni Gaudí. The bishop then in office was, like Gaudí, from Reus and was familiar with the architect's achievements, which is how he got the commission. Construction began in the year 1887 and the hand of Gaudí is very obvious in the finished result, although this is without doubt one of his lesser works. Inside there is now a valuable collection of religious art brought together under the name 'Museo de los Caminos' (museum of the pathways). You can also learn more about the constructional and decorative ideas which Gaudí put into practice.

The cathedral displays a mixture of styles which bear witness to the space of time over which it was built and to its subsequent remodellings. The main façade is now clearly Baroque, but inside you can see some Gothic sections

Foncebadón|1h20min|RabanaldelCamino|1h30min|ElGanso|55min|SantaCatalinadeSomoza|1h50min|**Astorga**

covering the earlier Romanesque parts, which are the most ancient. The cathedral dates from the mid-fifteenth century and has three altarpieces of great artistic value.

Between the Plaza Mayor and the cathedral lie the streets of the old town with their profusion of shops where the city's renowned confectionery may be purchased (see box on page 120). As there are steep climbs on the stages which lie ahead, you might want to invest in some since you will soon need the energy!

Murias de Rechivaldo – Santa Catalina de Somoza
1 h 50 min
Although you emerge from the close-knit streets of the old town only shortly after passing beside the cathedral, the route out of Astorga

Smiling pilgrims at El Ganso

The Way at Santa Catalina de Somoza

then takes you along comfortable, broad pavements which allow you to remain at a safe distance from the traffic. Furthermore, the Way is well marked. You soon pass by the village of Valdeviejas, on the right, and see, beside the road on the left, the renovated Ecce Homo chapel. A few hundred metres before reaching Murias de Rechivaldo you join a walkway.

The more ascetic pilgrims prefer to stay at the hostel in the small town of Murias rather than in Astorga, in order to keep away from the nightlife of that city.

After Murias the path becomes progressively steeper right to the end of the stage. You have already witnessed the change in the landscape. The plain of Castilla y León is behind us and a mountain range, Montes de León, now lies ahead. Although the climbs will not

Mesón Cowboy

El Ganso is just one more of the many small towns along the Way without any monument of note. However, every traveller stops to take a look at the Mesón Cowboy, a 'Wild West' bar so unusual that it appeared in one of the most amusing scenes of the French film *Peregrinos*, although this may have created the false impression that bars of this kind are common in Spain.

be too demanding, they are the first that you will have come to since the long-distant Montes de Oca.

Arrow markers made of stones and gravel point which way to go upon leaving Murias. A broad, well-maintained, rural track takes you to Santa Catalina de Somoza. There you can, if you wish, take a rest on benches placed in front of a series of great crosses. All of these were originally iron, made from the ore mined in the area, but those which had suffered most in the course of time have since been replaced with crosses made of wood.

Santa Catalina de Somoza – El Ganso
2 h 45 min

Ascending, gently but constantly, you come to El Ganso. You have reached what is, roughly, the half-way point of the stage and may wish to make a stop to rest and have something to eat. From here on you will have a steady climb until the end of the stage.

El Ganso – Rabanal del Camino
4 h 15 min

On leaving El Ganso you come to a pathway so narrow that it is difficult to place both feet side by side. Very shortly, however, it opens

This pilgrim, evidently undaunted by the additional weight, carries a Thermos flask of coffee and is happy to share its contents. Right: church of El Ganso.

Left: the church at Rabanal del Camino.
Above: drinking trough on the way up
to Foncebadón.

out considerably. Before reaching Rabanal you come to an oak wood. At this point you walk by a wire fence festooned with little wooden crosses hand-made by pilgrims. You then enter the well-kept town of Rabanal del Camino and pass by the church of Santa María (Saint Mary).

Many pilgrims choose to spend the night here, as the town is so welcoming. To do so, however, cuts the stage rather short. It is preferable not to leave so much of the remaining climb for the following day.

Rabanal del Camino – Foncebadón
5 h 35 min

This section is perhaps the most mountainous since the Pyrenean stages. The path zigzags through a wood of oaks and holm oaks with plentiful gorse. It generally stays away from the road, but has to cross it numerous times. Coming out of Rabanal you pass by the old public laundry and two well-made drinking troughs. The climb up to Foncebadón is constant and hard, with very few resting points.

Eating
All the towns on this stage have bar and restaurant facilities. Rabanal del Camino also has a grocery store, although by the time you reach that town you are coming towards the end of your day's journey. In general, bear in mind the plain is behind you and you have to walk uphill practically all day.

It is therefore advisable to carry foodstuffs that will give you a little more energy.

Sleeping
Only a couple of decades ago Foncebadón was abandoned and in ruins. Now it has three hostels and even a restaurant. This bears witness to the economic miracle that the

Way has worked. Domus Dei (no telephone) is the parish hostel. It opens from April to October. Monte Irago (telephone 0034 695 452 950) is private and opens all year. The convent hostel (telephone 0034 658 974 818) closes only in the harshest winter months, December and January.

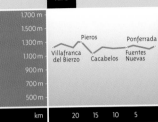

From Foncebadón to Ponferrada
The 'roof' of the Way

24.5 km • 6 h 30 min

Foncebadón – Cruz de Fierro
30 min

The first section of this stage is a stiff climb. However, as you did most of the uphill work on the preceding stage and the track is good and broad, it will take barely half an hour to reach the Cruz de Fierro (Iron Cross). This is a major milestone given that it marks the 'roof' of the Way, at a height of 1,500 m, although the slope is not the toughest one that the traveller has to tackle in the course of the pilgrimage.

The little iron cross mounted on a tall wooden post is not the original one. It replaces another

Distances from Manjarín

whose origins may have been many centuries more distant, as this was originally the site of a Roman altar dedicated to the god Mercury. At the base there is a mound of little stones left by pilgrims. It was a time-honoured custom for pilgrims to bring a stone from their home towns and drop it here. The act symbolized the deliverance from sin afforded by the pilgrimage. In recent decades, however, the essence of that custom has been lost, as most of the stones now come from just metres away. In addition, travellers have begun to leave all manner of 'votive offerings' and the base of the cross has consequently acquired an untidy look. It would be worthwhile reviving the original practice, so that the site no longer looks like a second-hand goods stall.

The area around the cross is well laid out. There is a sundial on which the pilgrim is the gnomon (the stationary arm that projects the shadow). There is also a small chapel and an extensive rest and picnic area for car parties and ramblers.

Cruz de Fierro and sundial

Ponferrada | 2 h | Molinaseca | 2 h | El Acebo | 2 h | Cruz de Fierro | 30 min | **Foncebadón**

You still have six hours' walk ahead. On clear days, however, the city of Ponferrada, the end of this section, can be seen from here.

Cruz de Fierro – Manjarín
1 h

The Cruz de Fierro is revered, to the extent that you may well see pilgrims praying on their knees beneath it. From here the path leads downward, but don't be misled into thinking that the rest of the stage will all be downhill. There is still some climbing to do. A well-kept walkway takes you to Manjarín in half an hour. The village is abandoned and in ruins, except for its peculiar hostel. Those with a keen interest in the Knights Templar will without doubt have noted this as a place to stop. The pennants and crosses bear witness to the efforts of the *hospitalero* to revive the tradition of that legendary order.

Coming to El Acebo and Riego de Ambros

Another icon of the village is the post bearing numerous wooden signs indicating the distance from here to other points on the planet. The signs which generally arouse most interest are those informing us that there are 70 kilometres to Galicia, 255 to Santiago and 295 to Finisterre.

The local hostel will provide a memorable experience for those who do not think basic means uncomfortable.

Manjarín – El Acebo
2 h 30 min

From Manjarín you take a mountain path which leads steadily upward to a pass forested with television and telephone masts. This could actually be just as high as the Cruz del Fierro, but it does not seem as high nor does it have the same mystique. The rest of the stage consists of a very lengthy downhill stretch, with just one short upturn, of the knee-punishing kind.

El Acebo – Riego de Ambros
3 h 15 min

Although the outline of this stage shows a frightening descent, it is in fact progressive. The track is stony, however, and therefore uncomfortable. There is also the risk of twisting an ankle and it is wise to take care. El Acebo is a small but well-kept town. Most of the houses have been restored and some old agricultural implements, now in disuse, decorate the streets and fields. There is a bar and a grocery store.

The river Maruelo at Molinaseca

On leaving the town you pass by a monument, painted in silver, to the memory of a bike pilgrim who died at this point. Generally speaking, cyclists may be tempted to take this descent at speed, but the track is narrow and dangerous. There is consequently a need to exercise restraint.

By now you will have observed that the style of architecture is changing significantly. Slate begins to take the place of tile, while the wooden balconies suggest a timber-producing area and a cooler climate. You have just entered the region of El Bierzo. This is one of the sections of the Way with the greatest character and it makes a pleasant transition between the austere Castille and the green and wooded Galicia.

You now have a half-hour long, steep, downhill walk on the road before coming to a track which bypasses the long bends in the road and so provides a more direct descent. This takes you to Riego de Ambros.

Riego de Ambros – Molinaseca
4 h 30 min

The Way has breathed new life into Riego de Ambros and, indeed, into all this valley, which now has a buoyant atmosphere, particularly in the high season. On leaving the town you have to cross a small gully flanked by leafy chestnuts. At this point the track levels off and you again come to

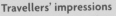

an ascent, albeit a short one. The path takes you through mountain scenery, with streams, woods and inclines. The arrows disappear at times, but if you come to an unmarked fork we should always take the path leading down towards the valley floor. Before reaching Molinaseca you at times find yourself walking down the dry bed of a stream, where the descent is very steep.

Molinaseca – Campo
5 h 30 min

It is not until you come to the river Maruelo and see the old town of Molinaseca on the left bank that the great descent of the day comes to an end. The two hours' walk which still lie ahead are essentially on the flat.

For twenty minutes you walk along a pavement which leads you out of Molinaseca and you then come to a broad, well-kept rural track running between vines to Campo. It may descend a little at times, but this is nothing compared with the stretch you have left behind, where the descent was over a thousand metres in all.

Campo – Ponferrada
6 h 30 min

Before reaching Ponferrada you again have to walk on tarmac. Cross the railway lines by means of a footbridge and then take the stone bridge over the river Sil. It is a little difficult to follow the signs to the hostel, but they reappear at a traffic roundabout.

The old town (top) and the Templar castle in Ponferrada

Eating
On this stage there is no bar or restaurant until you reach El Acebo. Subsequently, all the towns of a certain size have facilities. At Riego de Ambros and Molinaseca there are also shops. Ponferrada, the capital of El Bierzo, provides all the facilities you may need.

Sleeping
The parish hostel (telephone 0034 987 413 381) opens all year. Strangely, it is the only one there is. This is surprising, bearing in mind that Ponferrada is a medium-sized city and a stage end for practically all pilgrims. The hostel is, at all events, enormous (250 beds), although this has drawbacks as well as advantages. The city also has a good network of guest and boarding houses at a range of prices.

From Ponferrada to Villafranca del Bierzo
Ups and downs between vines

700 m
600 m   Pieros   Ponferrada
500 m Villafranca   Fuentes
400 m del Bierzo   Cacabelos   Nuevas
300 m
200 m

km   15   10   5   **21.1 km • 5 h 45 min**

Ponferrada – Columbrianos
1 h

After leaving the hostel head for the old town, where you will be passing beside some of the city's most prominent monuments. Take time to look at a few of the principal sights before moving on. You can afford to do so, given that the stage which lies ahead is neither long nor difficult.

One of the most emblematic monuments of Ponferrada is the Renaissance-style Torre del Reloj (Clock Tower), which stands over one of the gates in the wall. Passing beneath it you enter the rather dark, close world of the old town, although the Plaza Mayor provides a pleasant, spacious contrast. The city's most important temple is the Basilica de la Encina (Basilica of the Holm Oak), a Renaissance building dating from the end of the sixteenth century. Its name comes from the tree where the Knights Templar found a figure of the Virgin. According to the legend, the statue had been hidden in the hollow of a large tree trunk

centuries earlier to keep it safe from the invading Moors. There it remained, the hiding place forgotten, until one of the warrior monks, out cutting firewood, came across it. Other noteworthy buildings include the town hall and the Casa de los Escudos (House of Shields), beside the castle, which now houses the Radio Museum, a project promoted by the well-known radio journalist Luis del Olmo, who was born in Ponferrada. There is also the historic Real Cárcel (Royal Prison), which is now home to the Museum of El Bierzo.

Monument to the pilgrim at Villafranc

Most important of all, however, is the Templar castle. From the outside it

Pilgrims at Fuentes Nuevas

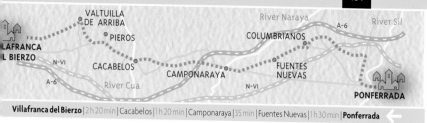

Villafranca del Bierzo | 2 h 20 min | Cacabelos | 1 h 20 min | Camponaraya | 35 min | Fuentes Nuevas | 1 h 30 min | **Ponferrada**

has rather an artificial look and gives the impression of being only a small fortress. However, once inside, (there is an admission fee), you can more fully appreciate the construction, which dates from the twelfth century. When the Knights Templar were given control of the castle they extended the original structure, thus ensuring its domination of the hill, the river Sil and the nearby plain.

The river Cúa at Cacabelos and pilgrims consulting the guidebook

There are many churches and fortresses along the Way of Saint James that are attributed to the Templars, but in the case of Ponferrada castle their role is fully documented. The extensions which the castle underwent in the course of the centuries and the erection of further installations inside the walls are well explained through information panels placed at the relevant points. The coats of arms of the various noble families who played a part in the management of the castle are displayed on one of the main walls. The castle was declared a historic artistic monument in 1924.

The castle is open to visitors from 11.00 to 14.00 and from 16.00 to 18.00 from Tuesday to Saturday. On Sundays and public holidays it opens mornings only. It is closed on Mondays.

Having thus taken a rewarding look at the monuments of Ponferrada, you should now take to the path. There are not many signs showing the way out of the city, but they are at least strategically placed. While you therefore ought not to get lost, you need to be more than usually attentive for the first half-hour, as you will come to a succession of traffic lights, crossroads and roundabouts where there is always the possibility of taking a wrong turn.

A bucolic scene at Valtuilla

A very characteristic region

El Bierzo is one of the great discoveries of the pilgrimage. Its character makes itself felt from the moment you arrive, as it is greener, more mountainous and the architecture has changed. In this region you also begin to see and hear signs of a different identity. *Gallego* (Galician) is the mother tongue of many of the inhabitants and it is here that you will first hear that language spoken.

Columbrianos – Fuentes Nuevas
1 h 30 min

You will realize that you are in Columbrianos and no longer within the limits of Ponferrada only when you see the sign bearing the name of the former. You are in an extensive residential area where one development follows another, with sports facilities appearing from time to time. Here the arrows appear more regularly, but pay attention when coming into Fuentes Nuevas: while this guide was being written, one of the marker stones that indicated a turning there was being practically swallowed up by the works on the construction of a new building. If

The Puerta del Perdón welcomes the pilgrim to Villafranca del Bierzo

you are in any doubt, remember that the Way crosses the town, leaving the road on which you entered the town to your right. The alternative, as always, is to ask a local for directions.

Fuentes Nuevas – Camponaraya
2 h 5 min

You leave Fuentes Nuevas to the left of the cemetery by way of a tarmacked track that leads you to a local road. Although there is very little traffic, the conditions are uncomfortable, as there is very little shoulder to the road and, in some places, none at all.

Camponaraya – Cacabelos
3h 25 min

You cross Camponaraya via an avenue, leading slightly uphill, where most of the town's facilities are to be found. There is a fountain and some benches where you can rest, but the slight inclines you have encountered up to this point should not have tired you out much. You may be feeling the heat, however, as there is little shade on this stage. Next, you cross the river Naraya and, shortly after a service station, take a bridge over the A-6 motorway. From this point the landscape becomes more rural and pleasanter. You walk between

Pilgrim leaving Villafranca via the bridge over the Burbia and (below) Villafranca castle

vines which provide the increasingly valued wine of El Bierzo. The terrain goes up and down, but the only difficulties for the traveller lie in the dust that the path throws up and the absence of shade. And so you come to Cacabelos.

Cacabelos – Pieros
4 h 5 min

After three hours or more of fairly level ground you come to a tough uphill stretch. The walkway is narrow and right beside the road. You pass Pieros without entering the town as such and at once come to a fork. Here you go to the right, towards Valtuilla.

Pieros – Valtuilla de Arriba
4 h 35 min

This alternative route makes the stage a little longer, but it has the advantage of crossing a pleasant landscape between apple trees and vines.

Valtuilla de Arriba – Villafranca del Bierzo
5 h 45 min

A gentle ascent taking about an hour brings you to the Puerta del Perdón (Door of Forgiveness). You are now in Villafranca del Bierzo.

Eating

All the towns along this stage, except Pieros and Valtuilla de Arriba towards the end, have bars, restaurants and grocery stores. It is therefore not difficult to decide where and when to eat, bearing in mind, furthermore, that the stage is not a long one.

Sleeping

Villafranca del Bierzo is a small city and has all the corresponding facilities. There are four hostels. You come to the first just before entering the built-up area. It is municipal (telephone 0034 987 542 680) and opens from March to November. Close by the Puerta del Perdón is the Ave Fénix hostel (telephone 0034 987 540 229), which opens all year and has won a very good name given the charm of the *hospitalero*

who runs it. Albergue Viña Femita (telephone 0034 987 542 490) is at calle Calvo Sotelo, 2. It opens from mid-January to mid-December. Lastly, on the outskirts (a ten-minute walk) there is the albergue de la Piedra (telephone 0034 987 540 260), which opens from March to November. The city also has a good network of guest and boarding houses at affordable prices.

From Villafranca del Bierzo to O Cebreiro
The uphill track out of León

27.5 km • 7 h 15 min

Villafranca del Bierzo – Pereje
1 h 20 min

The number of banks in Villafranca del Bierzo bears witness to the town's prosperity. Of more interest, however, are the outstanding buildings of the old quarter, such as the castle with its four round towers, the old convent of San Nicolás (Saint Nicholas) or the church of Santiago (Saint James) with its well-known Puerta del Perdón (Door of Forgiveness), which you passed by at the end of the preceding stage.

To leave Villafranca you go down a flight of steps from the centre, following the discreetly placed arrows, and take the bridge over the river Burbia. Outside the built-up area the signs disappear, but if you keep to the road which follows the river Valcarce you will be going in the right direction. In three kilometres

Pereje at the start of the day

you come to a crossroads. Here the hard shoulder, painted entirely in yellow, is separated from the main N-006A road by a concrete barrier. This should give the pilgrim a well-founded sense of safety. Whoever may seek a metaphor in the Way, in the sense that it is always close to the real world but moves in an orbit of its own, could find it here.

Beneath the rain in the woods of Trabadelo

Stall selling sticks in Ambasmestas.
Below: La Portela, at 190 km from
the end of the pilgrimage

When you reach Pereje take the time to have a look at the town, given that it is a fine example of the traditional architecture of El Bierzo.

Pereje – Trabadelo
2 h 10 min

Cross the road, carefully, and return to the 'yellow walkway'. It ascends more gently than it appears to. Vehicles roar past, but you should feel well protected by the barrier. Imposing chestnuts welcome you to Trabadelo, where you will pass a sawmill with great piles of cut timber around it.

Trabadelo – La Portela
3 h 10 min

From Trabadelo on the climb becomes steeper, although it does not compare to what awaits you in the second half of the day. The surroundings remain the same. You are close to the traffic but at the same time protected, while woods stretch out on either side.

La Portela – Ambasmestas
3 h 30 min

At the end of the yellow walkway you find yourself on a local road where there is neither traffic nor noise. You then come to Ambasmestas, a thoroughly rural village, where an enterprising local keeps a stall

alongside the Way selling staffs for pilgrims.

Ambasmestas – Vega de Valcarce
3 h 45 min

Passing beneath rather intimidating viaducts, you next come to Vega de Valcarce, a large town and the main one in the valley.

Reinvented *pallozas*

As it is the first Galician town along the French Way, O Cebreiro has witnessed a resurgence in recent years. Practically everybody has moved into the services sector. Even the traditional *pallozas*, round pre-Roman structures made of stone and thatch, formerly used for agricultural purposes and before that as dwellings, have in many cases been carefully restored and converted into private guest houses.

Vega de Valcarce – Ruitelán
4 h 25 min

You have now covered more than half the stage, but the hardest part is yet to come. Consequently, as Vega de Valcarce has many amenities, this may be the right time to take a break, have something to eat or buy provisions, as you will need stamina on the steep, uphill stretch you come to in the last eight kilometres of the stage.

Ruitelán – Las Herrerías
4 h 45 min

On the short walk between Ruitelán and Las Herrerías you may notice how the landscape in this area is changing fast. You are still in the region of Castilla y León, but the surroundings have already taken on a clearly Galician look and you start to see small villages where cattle and dairy farming are the main activities. You are entering a land of greenness and regular rainfall, in sharp contrast to the harsh, dry terrain of the past weeks. Las Herrerías stands beside the river Valcarce, which has accompanied the route all morning. Here you come to the foot of the pass you have to climb.

Las Herrerías – La Faba
5 h 45 min

You reach a leafy wood which affords protection from the sun or, as the case may be, the rain. As the trees cut off the horizon, it seems at first that you are not advancing, but when the route begins to zigzag and the effort becomes harder you realize that you are climbing fast. This is the toughest stretch of the stage.

For a kilometre you walk on tarmac and then come to a marker stone where a path leads off to the left. Although there are odd signs, perhaps placed there to promote some of the local bars or inns, this is the correct route. While flat at first, it then climbs

The church at O Cebreiro, where the Galician section of the Way begins

Traveller with the views from
O Cebreiro below him

steeply through the chestnut wood and gives practically no respite all the way to La Faba, which in turn perches on the hillside. The village has a fountain which will probably be very welcome.

La Faba – Laguna de Castilla
6 h 35 min
You have now left the wood and are not far from Laguna de Castilla. The incline ahead looks less severe, but unfortunately that is not the case. Grit your teeth while climbing bare terrain without shelter from the sun,

the wind or the rain. Finally you reach Laguna de Castilla, the last town in Castilla y León.

Laguna de Castilla – O Cebreiro
7 h 15 min
Behind the hill you find a sign telling you that you are entering the region of Galicia. Here the incline becomes gentler and in two kilometres you are in O Cebreiro, where there are splendid views over the valley.

Eating
This stage is a hard one, entailing an ascent of almost a thousand metres. Although your legs have covered hundreds of kilometres, they are unaccustomed to such sharp inclines. However, at least there are bars and restaurants in all the towns you pass through, although some of them may open late, or for shorter hours, outside the high season. There are, in addition, shops in Trabadelo, Ambasmestas, Vega de Valcarce, Ruitelán, Las Herrerías and La Faba.

Sleeping
The large network of hostels set up by the *Xunta* (regional government) of Galicia comes as a pleasant surprise

to the traveller. These hostels are well equipped, make a charge of only three euros and provide, for hygienic reasons, paper bottom sheets and pillowcases. The O Cebreiro hostel (telephone 0034 660 396 809) is at the end of the town on a windy promontory. There are also half a dozen private guest or boarding houses in the town.

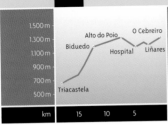

From O Cebreiro to Triacastela
Galicia from the heights

18 km • 4 h 55 min

O Cebreiro – Liñares
35 min

If, at the end of yesterday's climb, you did not have time to take a look at O Cebreiro, try and do so today before leaving. The architecture is elegant, the houses and *pallozas* are well restored and the church, which marks the starting point for the many pilgrims who only walk the Galician section of the Way, is pretty. In summer you may well find pilgrims sleeping under the shelter of its porch, as the accommodation available in the town is not always sufficient.

In the church, where the pilgrim's pass is issued to those starting from here, there is a chalice connected with a miracle which occurred in the early fourteenth century. When a man who had travelled a long disrance in hard weather to hear mass was treated with disdain by the local priest, the wine in the chalice turned to blood.

From now on the signs are in Galician

The route out of O Cebreiro is spectacular, providing views that extend for many kilometres all around. Green pastures and small villages dot the landscape below. A path leads you steadily downhill practically to Liñares. The path is marked, but if you don't find it just take the road instead. The distance is much the same, although obviously you have to pay attention to the traffic on the latter.

Liñares – Alto de San Roque
55 min

At Liñares, which is little more than a group of houses beside the road, you come to an unusual minimalist monument differing in style from those you have seen before. It consists of a simple iron rod, shaped to symbolize a staff and gourd, set in a rock alongside the Way.

After Liñares the markers take you to a track leading steeply uphill.

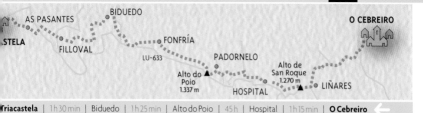

Ascent to Fonfría and chapel of Padornelo

For some minutes you walk through the edge of a wood where holly trees abound. You then come out at the pass of Alto de San Roque. You are 1,270 metres above sea level and the wind blows cold here. You have further climbs to face, however, before coming to the high point of the stage.

Alto de San Roque – Hospital
1 h 15 min

On leaving the pass behind you come to a twenty-minute stretch of alternating ascents and descents. None of them is very hard and the earth track is in good condition, but your legs may remind you of the demands of the previous day and of the hundreds of kilometres they have by

now covered. The village of Hospital has a charming, solidly built church crowned with an iron cross. The name Hospital is a reference to the medieval pilgrims' hospice which once stood here.

Hospital – Padornelo
1 h 55 min

From this point many pilgrims choose to follow the road to the next pass, as the distance is a little shorter. However, our recommendation is that you instead stay with the signs and so take a path which loses a little height but leads you through heather and rockrose. It crosses the village of Padornelo, where there is

Even the monument has to take precautions against the wind at Alto do Poio

Return to the past

On stage 25 the pilgrim walks through a rural world that has disappeared in other parts of the country. Many women, above all the older ones, dress entirely in black and cover their hair with a scarf. The villagers make their living raising cattle and dairy farming (the streets are full of the evidence of this!). The people are friendly and eager to talk, happy to see new faces from time to time.

an elongated chapel, every part of which is made of stone (see photograph on preceding page). The little cemetery is also worth a look.

Padornelo – Alto do Poio
2 h

The path turns steeply upward and you have a hard ten-minute climb to the windy Alto do Poio, where there is an enormous monument representing a pilgrim in medieval dress holding on to his hat. There is nothing figurative about this, as the area is certainly exposed. You are at a height of 1,310 m and the temperature tends to be fairly low here even in the summer.

Alto do Poio – Fonfría
2 h 45 min

This is today's summit, with views extending for several kilometres all around. You now face a 700 m descent, which will take over two hours and prove a hard test for the knees.

The path is well marked and runs three or four metres above the level of the road.

Fonfría – Biduedo
3 h 25 min

The fact that Fonfría now has a couple of rural guest houses would seem to show that the area has experienced some economic growth in recent years. From here the path

Traditional houses at Triacastela. On the preceding page: the church and the cemetery

moves progressively away from the road and into pasture land, although the road always remains in sight. There is no shade here nor protection from the wind and the descent is now becoming steeper.

Biduedo – Filoval
4 h 5 min

On this stretch the path is almost good enough to be called a magic carpet. Triacastela, lying on the floor of the valley, is now in sight.

Filoval – As Pasantes
4 h 25 min

As Pasantes is, like most, an agricultural village. Old chestnut trees line the route here.

As Pasantes – Triacastela
4 h 55 min

On emerging from the wooded area you come to the lowest point on the day's stage. As you enter Triacastela you reach the hostel immediately.

Eating

This stage is short in terms of distance and time. Even so, you find bars and restaurants in all the towns and villages you pass through. This is useful bearing in mind the changeable nature of the weather in Galicia. Grocery shops may be found only at Liñares and Alto do Poio.

Sleeping

If you wish to stay at the Xunta de Galicia hostel (telephone 0034 982 548 087) you should not go into the built-up area of Triacastela. That hostel is located in a meadow at the entrance to the town. It is well equipped and subject to the same rules as all the others run by the regional government. Barely fifty metres away there is a bar where you

can have dinner and you only need to stroll for five minutes to find the range of services that Triacastela has to offer, which is very comprehensive. Although the first part of the town may look a little dull, when you come to the area where the road crosses you find shops, banks, boarding houses and even a camp site.

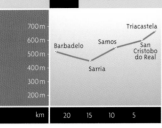

From Triacastela to Barbadelo
The 'Escorial' of Galicia

22.5 km • 6 h

Triacastela – Santo Cristobo do Real
55 min

Evening conversation in the hostels often turns to the stages which lie ahead. This stage is one of those most frequently discussed, as the question of whether to take the Samos or the San Xil route arises. The second of the two mainly follows the historic French Way to Santiago de Compostela and, in addition, is the shorter by some five kilometres. However, those who take it will miss one of Galicia's most prominent religious monuments. It is for this reason that we recommend the Samos route. Even though it is the longer of the two, stage 26 is in

The time to decide whether to go via San Xil or via Samos

any event short, both in hours and in kilometres. Furthermore, it is considerably flatter, as it avoids the Riocabo pass. Although most pilgrims take their decision beforehand, you don't have to commit yourself until five minutes after starting out. When you leave Triacastela, you come to the twin signs (see photograph on this page) inviting you to choose one route or the other.

At the end of the main street of Triacastela you turn to the left and leave the houses behind. At this point you need to pay attention. The road ascends to the left, but if you were to follow it you would go seven kilometres out of your way and have to cross a pass which is

The mighty monastery of Samos justifies our parting company with the historic Way for a day

tiring in both the ascent and the descent. To your right there is an earth track with a sign indicating Santo Cristobo do Real. This is the path you should take. It leads down to the floor of the valley and there, for a little longer than three kilometres, you have your first taste of what is to mark the tone of the day: wooded terrain with rivers and streams and cows grazing nearby. You are entering the land of the *corredoiras*, local wall-lined pathways, which characterize this part of the region.

A few hundred metres before reaching Santo Cristobo do Real you come out onto the road. There is a bend with barely any hard shoulder and you have to pay attention to the traffic. Very soon, however, you come to the small town, where a bar may be open if it is the high season or not too early in the day. You then go back down towards the river and return to the path.

Santo Cristobo do Real – Samos
2h 10 min

You now come to what are perhaps the five most spectacular kilometres of the Way on its passage through Galicia. First, you find yourself in a deep wood, where the pathways are carpeted with leaves and fallen chestnuts, the walls of the *corredoira* are covered with moss and there are limpid streams. The ground is soft,

Sarria, the second largest city of Galicia (after Santiago)

the terrain flat and the walking therefore easy all the way to Samos.

The path suddenly comes to a clearing from where you see the road and the top of the dome of the monastery. Advancing just 400 m we follow a bend and are confronted with the dramatic vision of the monastery of Samos. It is known as the 'Escorial' of Galicia, with reference to the great monastery of San Lorenzo de El Escorial in the province of Madrid.

The group of buildings, standing close beside the river Sarria, has an almost fortified look and is very imposing. On walking around the structure and coming to the main façade you can appreciate the equally impressive architectural details. There is a Baroque doorway with two horizontal and three vertical sections which has the unusual characteristic of being finished horizontally at the top. The stairway leading up to it is reminiscent, on a smaller scale, of the one in the plaza del Obradoiro in Santiago de Compostela. One of the cloisters inside is among the most spacious in Spain, with sides of over fifty metres. A statue of Father Benito Feijoo presides over it. There are also starred domes and valuable frescos.

The Benedictine monks take care of the upkeep and also provide accommodation for pilgrims. Those who can afford the time will do well to spend the night here, where they may continue to admire the architectural delights of Samos and enjoy the tranquillity of the surroundings at the end of the day.

Land of witches

There are sensational landscapes to be enjoyed on each of the three days we spend walking through the province of Lugo, but stage 26 has particular charm, given that it runs through deep, leafy chestnut woods with babbling streams. The mists and shadows may from time to time remind us that we are in a territory where *meigas* (witches) traditionally hold sway.

Samos – Sarria
3 h 55 min

Understandably, travellers tend to spend some time at Samos. If you want to catch up a little, you can take an unofficial walkway, created by the continuous passage of pilgrims, beside the road to Sarria. It is shorter and more even than the path running through the wood. Sarria is an important city, second in size, within Galicia, only to Santiago. Although it offers all the necessary services, it is still a bit

The church at Barbadelo is well worth a visit. The photograph shows a detail of the doorway

View from the municipal hostel at Barbadelo

early to stop and you should therefore continue for two more hours to Barbadelo.

Sarria – Barbadelo
6 h

After crossing Sarria you walk sharply downward past the cemetery and there take a pathway. You have to cross the railway line, walk through an old wood and subsequently climb a slope. When you come again to flat terrain the stage is not yet finished. You still have a fair stretch to cover before reaching your destination.

Eating

Stage 26 is very short and, by the route proposed, largely flat. Even so, you should take some basic supplies with you when leaving Triacastela. In the high season some roadside and village bars are open, but their opening hours tend to be very irregular for most months of the year. Provisions can be obtained at Samos and, particularly, at Sarria, but the latter is quite close to the end of the stage.

Sleeping

There are three hostels in Barbadelo. The municipal albergue de Barbadelo (telephone 0034 660 396 814) is run by the regional government. It is small but inviting and opens all year. It has a kitchen, but there is no grocery store in the village. Dinner and breakfast may be had at a bar/restaurant barely 200 m away. Albergue A Casa de Carmen (telephone 0034 982 532 294) is at San Silvestre Barbadelo, 3. It opens all year. Albergue O Pombal (telephone 0034 686 718 732) is just 100 m away from the municipal hostel. It opens from April to November. Private accommodation is also available in the village.

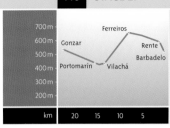

From Barbadelo to Gonzar
A psychological frontier

22.6 km • 6 h 20 min

Barbadelo – Rente
20 min

The municipal hostel in Barbadelo is in a marvellous location. The small building, an old schoolhouse, stands at the top of a sloping, grassy meadow where a great tree looks out over the surrounding countryside. It is worthwhile taking a walk to look at the little church and the adjacent cemetery. The capitals of the Roman-  esque doorway of the temple are decorated with scenes from the Bible and of the daily life of the people of Lugo in the Middle Ages. It is not easy to visit the interior, as the church is open only when the priest is present and he has a number of parishes to look after. The cemetery is an excellent place to discover interesting aspects of the traditional way of life.

Rente – Brea
1 h 25 min

When you are ready to leave walk up the track that leads to the 'centre' of Barbadelo. It is no more than a cluster of houses. As is common in this area, however, there are other small neighbourhoods, belonging to the village, in the vicinity. You at once come to a local road which is rarely used. What traffic there is moves slowly and you may there-fore walk calmly through a land-scape where cattle farming is clearly the main industry. The

The track to Brea. On the right, the 100 km marker stone.

salient features of the landscape are pastures and small herds, with oak trees here and there.

It takes no more than a quarter of an hour to cross Rente. From now until the end of the day you will be coming to *corredoira* after *corredoira* in an idyllic landscape of stone walls and moss and ancient trees. If you look over the walls you will see rich pasture, although there seem to be fewer cows and horses here.

There are not many signs to help you identify the villages you pass through, which are generally deserted. However, if you pay attention to the map you will see that you have come through Mercado and are entering Peruscallo. You now come to a stretch where the route follows the bed of a little stream and large slabs have been laid so that the traveller may walk above the level of the water.

At Brea we come to the first bar on this stage.

Brea – Ferreiros
2 h 15 min

The section between Brea and Ferreiros is one of particular significance for the pilgrim. It is not that the landscape changes, but on leaving the first of these villages you encounter one of the stones put in place by the Lugo provincial council to mark the Way. It tells

A small *horreo* (raised granary) at Vilachá

you that the distance remaining to Santiago de Compostela is precisely 100 km. That will take you barely three and a half days.

Some respectful pilgrims have placed pebbles on top of the marker. Others, unfortunately, were unable to resist the base temptation to paint it with scrawled messages of no interest to anyone and it has, as a result, been sadly defaced.

Ferreiros – Vilachá
3 h 50 min

The baser side of human instinct is quickly forgotten when you find

The river Miño

Today's stage is highly symbolic. The pilgrim passes by the 100 km (distance to Santiago) marker stone and also crosses the river Miño where the construction of the Belasar dam caused the pretty town of Portomarín to be relocated. The Galician landscape is inspiring and your legs may seem to gather renewed strength, despite the kilometres they have covered.

yourself in an enchanted world where moss envelops the stones and gives the land a touch of emerald green which gleams in the sunbeams filtering through the foliage. The surroundings are so beautiful that you may not have noticed that since you left Barbadelo you have been ascending constantly. It is at Ferreiros that you reach the high point of the stage, at 700 metres above sea level. From here you come first to a series of ascents and descents, extending over a couple of kilometres, and then to a steep downward slope entailing an abrupt 300-metre descent.

Half an hour before you come to Vilachá the landscape opens up and you have panoramic views of the rolling hills and the valley, together with the town of Portomarín. You then return, however, to the *corredoiras* which take us into Vilachá, an entirely farming-based town.

Vilachá – Portomarín
4 h 20 min

It is just half an hour from Vilachá to Portomarín, downhill and mostly

A porticoed street and the church in Portomarín

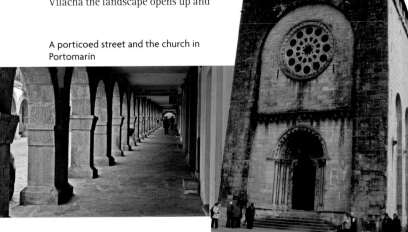

on tarmac. The route takes you down to the Belasar dam on the river Miño, across the bridge, up a majestic flight of steps crowned with an arch, into a pretty porticoed street lined with shops and finally to the church.

Portomarín was relocated when the dam was built. Nobody would think so, however, as the town gives the impression of having always stood on this hill. The church of San Nicolás (Saint Nicholas) resembles a castle, more vertical than horizontal and crenellated at the top. The principal feature of the front of the building is a large rose window. Beneath it a short flight of steps leads up to a Romanesque doorway.

Portomarín – Cortapezas
5 h
To leave Portomarín you have to walk back down the hill. The arrows guide you to a footbridge and, once on the other side of the Miño, along a woodland path lined with heather and gorse. Subsequently, on reaching Cortapezas, you take a walkway.

Cortapezas – Gonzar
6 h 20 min
On this stretch you find yourself walking close to the road some of the time and at others through a fragrant pine wood from which vehicles can neither be seen nor heard. The route leads slightly upward and, as you near the end of the stage, takes you through a picnic area. You then see the first signs for the hostels at Gonzar.

The little church at Gonzar with its iron cross

Eating
From the time you enter Galicia be aware that you will be passing through a large number of hamlets consisting of little groups of houses without any centre as such. Not surprisingly, many of these villages have no services for the traveller. Although, on this stage, Brea and Ferreiros have a bar/restaurant, there is no grocery store until you reach Portomarín. Gonzar, the end of this stage, has no shops.

Albergue Municipal de Gonzar
(a 100 metros)

Café Bar Restaurante
(a 100 metros)

Sleeping
Gonzar has a good public hostel (telephone 0034 982 157 840). It is large, has all the conveniences and is right beside the Way. It also has facilities for parking bicycles. There is also a private hostel, Casa García (telephone 0034 982 157 842), just beside the church. Both open all year.

700m
600m — Alto del Rosario — Alto de Ligonde
500m — Melide — Palas — Airexe
400m — de Rei — Gonzar
300m — Leboreiro
200m

km 25 20 15 10 5

From Gonzar to Melide
The first eucalyptuses

27.2 km • 7 h 20 min

Gonzar – Castromaior
20 min

The route out of Gonzar is easy. Leave the hostel, which stands on the Way itself, turn left and advance up a steep local road with little or no traffic. In twenty minutes you come to Castromaior, where you find the first cluster of eucalyptuses. You will be seeing this tree, native to Australia, uninterruptedly from here on, as in the past decades it has been planted by the thousand to supply the paper industry.

An exceptionally high *horreo* (raised granary) at Castromaior

Castromaior – Hospital de la Cruz
55 min

This is a stage with many climbs, but these first kilometres require most effort. There is a fairly stiff climb up to Ventas de Narón. The walkway is stony and rather uncomfortable but at least it is a certain distance from the road. You can't see the cars, although you do hear the hum of traffic. The village of Hospital de la Cruz takes its name from an old pilgrims' hospice, which still stands. There is a hostel but don't head towards it unless you need to, since you could lose sight of the markers, which are few and a little unclear.

The *crucero* (wayside cross) of Lameiros and detail of the skulls carved on the base

Melide | 3h35min | Palas de Rei | 1h35min | Airexe | 1h50min | Castromaior | 20min | Gonzar

Hospital de la Cruz – Ventas de Narón
1 h 15 min

On this stretch the climb becomes steeper, testing the legs of the pilgrim which, although by now very used to hard work, may be approaching the limit of their resistance after four weeks of constant effort. Coming to the top of the earth track, you cross a bridge over the main road to Ourense and take a pilgrim walkway, now leading downhill, to Ventas de Narón.

Ventas de Narón – Airexe
2 h 10 min

You now come to one of the most attractive and interesting sections of the stage. On leaving Ventas de Narón you walk along the verge of the road and may feel like you are on or beside a pavement, as slabs of granite have been placed between the road itself and the path. The route leads steadily upward to the pass of Ligonde. The high point, 756 metres, is marked by a stone, but it is not easy to spot just by looking. Descending from the pass you come first to the little village of A Previsa and then see, on the left, the impressive but disquieting cross of Lameiros, sheltered by a great oak, which warrants a

View from the pass of Ligonde (top) and a *cabaceiro* (small thatched granary) at Leboreiro

close look. The very worn base bears signs relating to death, while at the cross the figure of the Virgin makes reference to maternity and so to the creation of life. Here pilgrims have left painted stones, together with messages written on paper which the rain gradually washes away.

Airexe – Alto del Rosario
3 h 10 min

The 'pavement' continues to Airexe, where a stone cross greets you at the point of

entry while behind there stands a Romanesque church. The setting is typically Galician. On leaving the village you come to woodland paths. The trees are mainly eucalyptuses, but there are also some fine specimens of oak and beech which have withstood the invader from 'down under'. A series of short, sharp inclines takes you to Alto del Rosario, where there is a distance marker stone. The main road runs close by, but dense gorse keeps the vehicles out of sight.

The Alto del Rosario pass marks a turning point on the stage. Although still walking on rolling terrain, you will descend steadily until you come to the river Pambre and subsequently enter the province of A Coruña.

Alto del Rosario – Palas de Rei
3 h 45 min

Walking downhill, cross the village of Avenostre, a small farming community similar to the many others you have seen on the way through the province of Lugo. Shortly afterwards you come to Palas de Rei which, in contrast, is a large town with many services. There you go

past the church of San Tirso (Saint Thyrsus) and then head sharply down towards the valley of the Pambre.

Palas de Rei – San Xulián del Camiño
4 h 35 min

On this stretch you once again find yourself on very pleasant paths running gently up and down through eucalyptus-scented woods. However, before reaching the small but pretty village of San Xulián del Camiño you have to cross a marshy area. Large slabs have been laid down to help the traveller keep clear of the mud, but even so it will be hard to avoid getting your boots wet at times.

The river Furelos flows quietly by the town from which it takes its name

Granite sign in Melide. Right: the chapel of San Roque (Saint Roch)

San Xulián del Camiño – Casanova
5 h 10 min

The terrain is still marshy and you have to jump from slab to slab to cross the brooks and avoid the mud, but the village of Casanova is not far away.

Casanova – Leboreiro
5 h 55 min

It takes three quarters of an hour to reach Leboreiro, the first town in the province of A Coruña. Of particular interest are its paved street and *cabaceiro* (thatched granary).

Leboreiro – Melide
7 h 20 min

From this point onwards the surroundings become more industrial. Although you are walking on an earth track, there are sheds and factories on both sides practically all the way to the medieval bridge of Furelos. Finally, you come to the rather dull ascent to Melide.

Eating

Travellers who enjoy having 'a little something' in different bars or taverns will be in their element on this stage, as no fewer than ten of the towns or villages through which you pass have a bar and restaurant. However, those who prefer to organize their own picnic should be warned that shops can only be found in Palas de Rei, more than halfway along the stage. It is, at all events, a good idea to work up an appetite before reaching Melide, as the town is famous for its *pulperías* (octopus restaurants).

Sleeping

Melide is a town of a certain size with all the

facilities that the traveller needs. The municipal hostel (telephone 0034 660 396 822) is near the town hall. It opens all year. There is also the Albergue O Apalpador (telephone 0034 679 837 969) at calle San Antonio, 23. It is also open all year. Those who like more privacy and are prepared to pay market prices will find half a dozen guest or boarding houses in the town. Their rates are in general moderate.

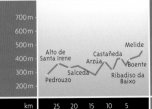

From Melide to Pedrouzo
Approaching our journey's end

28 km • 7 h 30 min

Melide – Boente
1 h 10 min

The route out of Melide is well marked. From the municipal hostel the arrows lead you sharply downward to the San Martiño road. You pass by the cemetery and also by the Romanesque church of Santa María (Saint Mary).

Once out of the built-up area you come to a wood of tall eucalyptuses interspersed with broader oaks. The terrain rises and falls and will basically continue thus throughout the day. The first three kilometres of the stage are gentle, but the inclines will subsequently become steeper. The overall changes in height are not very significant, but the gradients are taxing. Furthermore, the stage is a long one. Your body has already taken a lot of punishment and rush

to finish, now that the end approaches, could have unfortunate consequences. It is actually better, on this stage, to pause for a rest more frequently than you may have done in the preceding days.

Boente – Castañeda
1 h 45 min

Boente, a very small village, stands beside the road. The river of the same name is almost a hundred metres lower down. Descend to the river, cross it and then climb the other side. On this stretch, particularly, the climbs are very steep. Although it is only half an hour to Castañeda, a good deal of effort is required.

Castañeda – Ribadiso da Baixo
2 h 25 min

From Navarre on, the Way of Saint James runs from east to west. Given that on this last section the rivers run from north to south, you have no alternative but to cross them perpendicularly, which normally entails going down and up slopes. Although the watercourses are often in practice no more than unnamed streams, each one that has to be crossed calls for an additional effort on the part of the traveller. The last half-hour's walk to Ribadiso da Baixo differs, as it is on tarmac. The village is very

The gentle path to Salceda

RIBADISO
DA BAIXO   River Boente

ARZÚA

UZO   SALCEDA   N-547

CASTAÑEDA   BOENTE

RÚA   N-547   CASTAÑEDA   MELIDE

River Iso

Pedrouzo | 1h50min | Salceda | 2h40min | Arzúa | 1h50min | Boente | 1h10min | **Melide**

Mists around Pedrouzo

small, but it might be a good idea to pause a little here before taking on the steep incline leading to Arzúa.

Ribadiso da Baixo – Arzúa
3 h

It is a stiff climb all the way to the next town, as you will quickly realize. You are walking on tarmac, which makes the stretch doubly tiring, as the soles of your boots will have less grip than they would on an earth track. At least the distance is short. Arzúa is a fairly large town with all the services that the pilgrim may require. One

Well-looked-after granary at Ribadiso da Baixo

drawback, though, is that the built-up area is rather sprawling and for a full half-hour you find yourself dealing with crossroads and traffic lights and stepping off and onto pavements. You also have to pay attention to the traffic.

Even though you have not yet covered half the day's walking, you have to make certain decisions in Arzúa. You have to decide whether to break the journey here and whether to eat here or buy supplies for later. Bear in mind that, although you will be passing through typical farming hamlets, you will not see another bar or shop for almost three hours once you leave Arzúa.

Arzúa – Salceda
5 h 40 min
Getting out of Arzúa is a slow process. Once again you face a long and tedious series of crossings, traffic lights and avenues before finally leaving the buildings behind. The reward, however, is the woodland path which you then come to. Here the trail takes you up and down beneath the shade of the scented eucalyptuses. At times stone walls separate the path from pasture. At others it is bordered only by the vegetation. Almost without realizing, you leave behind the little villages of Pergontuño, Calzada and Calle Boavista.

The road generally lies to the left, but at times the path moves so far away from it that you do not even hear the hum of the traffic. It is to be noted that the A Coruña provincial council has done a good job in marking the pathway with stones every half-kilometre.

Salceda stands at a height of close to 300 m above sea level. Here you will once again find bars, restaurants and shops. There is a stretch of one and a half kilometres where you have to walk along the hard shoulder of the road. This is a particularly dangerous section, where drivers all

Carrying on
You know how many days you have spent so far and how much time you still have available. Consequently, on this penultimate stage, it is not unusual to find that people have made or are making plans to go farther, often to Finisterre, the goal closest to hand, or to more distant places such as Fatima in Portugal. Moreover, ever increasing numbers of pilgrims opt to walk back home along the Way in the opposite direction.

too often take insufficient care and the vehicles move at high speeds. It is therefore necessary to be more than usually attentive. As you draw close to Alto de Santa Irene you come to a crossroads that you have to negotiate with care. You then advance, keeping close to the edge of the tarmac, until the arrows lead you off the road.

Salceda – Alto de Santa Irene
6 h 40 min
Although Alto de Santa Irene is a pass, strangely the route does not subsequently go downward. The ascent continues up to the village of Rua.

Alto de Santa Irene – Rua
7 h 5 min
Rua stands on the flat and your legs therefore have some respite while

A fountain where you can take a rest

you are crossing the village. However, as soon as you leave the last house behind the climb begins afresh.

Rua – Pedrouzo
7 h 30 min
It takes less than half an hour to cover the distance between Rua and the day's destination. Once you reach the outskirts of Pedrouzo you should start to be on the watch for the municipal hostel, as it is easily missed. When you come to the post office you will see a ramp leading down. At the bottom is the hostel, just below the level of the street. If you find yourself walking along the main street of the town (which is in fact just a continuation of the road) for more than a couple of minutes, you have overshot.

The official name of the town is Pedrouzo, but everybody calls it Arca, as that is the name of the parish to which it belongs. To make matters even more complicated, the name of the district, which comprises this and other parishes, is O Pino. As Pedrouzo has become the

The centre of Arzúa (top) and notice in Boente warning us 'not to touch the door or the cat'

last stage destination prior to Santiago for almost everyone, its fame has grown throughout Galicia. In the evenings it is thronged with pilgrims making preparations for the great day. You are less than 20 kilometres from your goal.

Eating
This stage is as liberally sprinkled with little hamlets as the preceding ones. Once again, however, many of them have no facilities. Even so, no fewer than seven of the larger villages you come to have at least a bar or restaurant. For those who prefer a picnic, Boente, Castañeda, Arzúa and Salceda have shops. So you have plenty of choice.

Sleeping
Albergue de Arca do Pino, the public hostel (telephone 0034 660 396 826), is to the left of the road at the entrance to the town near the post office. It is rather hidden away, down a ramp. It tends to be quite noisy, given the exuberance of the pilgrims on the verge of accomplishing their goal. There are three other hostels. Albergue Porta de Santiago (telephone 0034 981 511 103) at Av. Lugo, 11 is open all year.

Albergue Edreira (telephone 0034 981 511 365) at rúa da Fonte, 19 opens from March to October (although it will also take advance bookings for November and December). Albergue O Burgo (telephone 0034 630 404 138) at Av. Lugo, 47 (by the service station) opens all year. Many travellers have by now had enough of communal dormitories. In Pedrouzo you will find three boarding houses offering decent service at moderate prices.

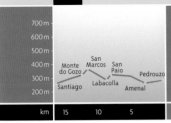

From Pedrouzo to Santiago de Compostela
Embracing the saint

16.6 km • 4 h 25 min

Pedrouzo – Tunnel
45 min

To leave Pedrouzo you walk up the main street for three or four minutes until you come to signs pointing to the schools and the football ground. Very soon you leave the houses behind and enter a wood where dappled native species mingle with tall eucalyptuses which scent the area and cover the path with their leaves and shreds of bark. The terrain is basically flat and will tend to remain that way for most of the stage.

The comfortable, earth path runs in and out of the wood and finally leads towards the main N-547. About a kilometre short of it you come to a tarmac surface and then to a tunnel which takes you safely under the road.

Tunnel – Labacolla
1 h 25 min

Pass by two groups of houses which have no name signs. Only by consulting

Omnipresent symbols in Santiago

the map do you learn that these hamlets are called San Antón and Amenal. In the second of the two you have to cross the watercourse of the same name and then, once again, the N-547. Subsequently you come to the village of Cimadevila and then to a climb between groups of eucalyptuses, leading towards the pass of Labacolla. The climb, although lengthy, poses no difficulty

Monument erected on Monte do Gozo to commemorate the visit of the Pope in 1992

Santiago de Compostela | 1 h 5 min | Monte do Gozo | 55 min | Vilamaior | 1 h | Alto de Labacolla | 1 h 25 min | **Pedrouzo**

and only goes up about a hundred metres in all.

The path takes you to the left of an enormous traffic junction and then moves progressively away from the tarmac along a slope screened with high gorse bushes. Here the ground is clayey and tends to be a little slippery. Coming to a stretch which rises and falls gently, you pass by Labacolla airport, to our left, and head for the village of San Paio. Next is Labacolla itself, which has bars and restaurants.

Labacolla – Vilamaior
2h 25 min
From Labacolla take a local road, running slightly upward, to Vilamaior. It lies parallel to the main road (which has now become the N-634) to the right. You can hear the hum of the vehicles there and at times even see them, but there is practically no traffic. The walk is therefore pleasant enough,

Marker stone at Labacolla pass

although the landscape has no remarkable features.

Vilamaior – San Marcos
3 h 10 min
From the village of Vilamaior take a gentle but constant ascent to San Marcos, with its scattered clusters of houses.

Galician cemeteries
The cemeteries in Galicia are magnificent, just as they are in many other rural areas in Spain. From O Cebreiro on you will see them in great number, peaceful, well laid out, well kept and often displaying noteworthy examples of funerary art. The last one you come to is at Labacolla, where the stonework is outstanding.

San Marcos – Monte do Gozo
3 h 20 min

You will have barely entered the village when the yellow arrows point you in the direction of the last remaining metres to Monte do Gozo. You reach the top in a matter of minutes, but the vegetation prevents you from seeing the enormous concrete monument erected there, to commemorate the visit of Pope John Paul II in 1992, until you are almost beside it. It stands to the left of the path and is in the form of a truncated pyramid whose four sides bear allegorical pictures. It is surmounted by a wrought-metal sculpture and a cross. Around it are some austere stone benches.

Taking photographs in plaza del Obradoiro

Leaving aside the question of the artistic merit of this work and of its suitability to the site, it is in any event clear that Monte do Gozo is no longer what it was for the medieval pilgrim. The Spanish word *gozo* means 'joy' and this name was given to the hill because it was from here that the pilgrim could first see the spires of the cathedral of Santiago de Compostela. Nowadays the view is obscured first by a wood and then by the urban sprawl of the Galician capital. Only from the edge of the earth platform on which the monument stands can you still see it. However, even though the circumstances have changed, many pilgrims still like to observe the ritual of former times and so, like their predecessors, spend the night here, wash their clothes, attend to their appearance and so enter the city of the Saint well groomed. We, however, recommend you carry on, in the more modern fashion, downhill towards Santiago.

The magnificent old town of Santiago de Compostela on a sunny day

Monte do Gozo – Santiago de Compostela
4 h 25 min

After the giant monument you come to the equally huge hostel complex built to cater for the needs of pilgrims in the summer. It is ugly, but its existence is understandable in light of the popularity that the Way has gained in recent years. Approaching the city, you come to a transitional section which is more urban than industrial and then to the sign which tells you that you are entering the outskirts of Santiago.

In plaza de San Pedro you pass by a stone cross announcing the closeness of the cathedral. As you walk downward, following golden scallop shells encrusted in the ground, so your emotions surge, reaching their height as you come finally to the great plaza del Obradoiro dominated by the Baroque façade of the cathedral. It is a moment for smiles and embraces.

The time has come to enter the cathedral (see page 162), see the Pórtico de la Gloria (which may no longer be touched) and embrace the statue of the saint. A pilgrimage never to be forgotten thus comes to its conclusion.

A pilgrim lies down in plaza del Obradoiro so as to savour the moment of arrival

Eating
As this stage is short, most pilgrims plan to eat in Santiago itself. For those who get up late or walk slowly, however, there are bars, restaurants and shops at Labacolla, San Marcos and Monte do Gozo.

Sleeping
Santiago de Compostela has seven hostels. San Lázaro (telephone 0034 981 571 488) is open all year. Seminario Menor La Asunción (telephone 0034 881 031 768) at calle Belvis s/n opens from March to November. Acuario (telephone 0034 981 575 438) opens from March to November. Santo Santiago (telephone 0034 657 402 403) at rúa do Valiño, 3 opens all year. Mundoalbergue (telephone 0034 696 448 737) at calle San Clemente, 26 opens all year. O Fogar de Teodomiro (telephone 0034 981 582 920) at Plaza de Algalia de Arriba, 3 (just off Plaza Cervantes) opens all year. Jaime García Rodríguez (telephone 0034 981 587 324) at rúa de Moscova s/n opens from April. Some pilgrims like to follow the medieval custom of spending the night at the hostel on Monte do Gozo (telephone 0034 981 558 942) and coming down to Santiago in the morning. Santiago also has a multitude of hotels and boarding houses for all tastes and budgets. There are travellers who consider, on reaching their destination, that they have earned a night at the *parador* in plaza del Obradoiro itself.

Santiago de Compostela
The reward for your effort

Cathedral

The pilgrim is expected to perform certain rituals inside the cathedral. Upon entering, look to the right, where you will see the triple portal known as the Pórtico de la Gloria, which represents the story of salvation. In accordance with tradition, after their long journey pilgrims used to kneel before

the column bearing the representation of the Tree of Jesse and rest a hand on it. This went on for centuries, to the extent that the stone came to show evident signs of wear. Now, therefore, it is preserved behind railings and contact may be no more than visual. It is questionable whether that column is actually more valuable because of its artistic qualities or because, for a thousand years, it has been stroked by the hands of the millions of people who have knelt before it.

Pilgrim going over his plans after reaching plaza del Obradoiro

Next go up the staircase leading to the chamber where the image of the apostle presides over the main nave. The pilgrim embraces the statue from behind, thanking the saint for the protection afforded during the long journey. Beneath the altar, in a silver reliquary, lie the relics of the saint. Those who set off early on the last stage may be in time to attend the pilgrim's mass (12.00). The *compostela* (certificate of accomplishment) is issued by the Pilgrim's Office, which is behind plaza de los Caballos.

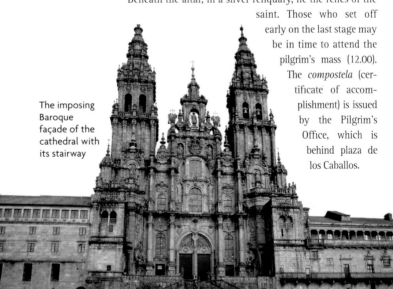

The imposing Baroque façade of the cathedral with its stairway

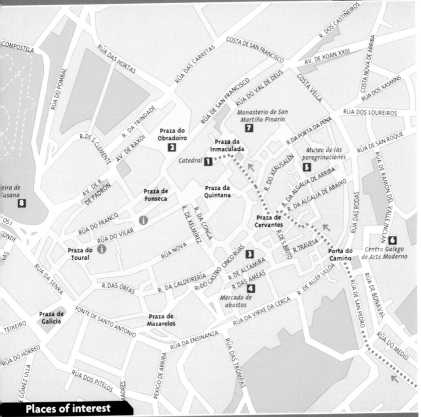

RÚA DAS HORTAS · RÚA DAS CARRETAS · COSTA DE SAN FRANCISCO · R. DOS CASTIÑEIROS · AV. DE XOAN XXIII · COSTA NOVA DE ARRIBA · RÚA DOS XASMINS · RÚA DE SAN FRANCISCO · RÚA DO VAL DE DEUS · COSTA VELLA · RÚA DOS LOUREIROS · RÚA DO POMBAL · R. DA TRINDADE · R. DE S. CLEMENTE · AV. DE RAXOI · R.DA PORTA DA PENA · RÚA DE SAN ROQUE · RÚA DE RAMÓN DEL VALLE INCLÁN · AV. DE R. DE PADRÓN · R. DO XERUSALEN · R. DA ALGALIA DE ARRIBA · R. DA ALGALIA DE ABAIXO · RÚA DO FRANCO · RÚA DO VILAR · R. DE XELMIREZ · R. DA CONGA · RÚA NOVA · R. DE S. BIETO · R.TRAVESA · RÚA DAS RODAS · RÚA DE BONAVAL · RÚA DE SAN PEDRO · RÚA DA SENRA · R. DA CALDEIRERÍA · R.DO CASTRO CINCO RÚAS · R. DE ALTAMIRA · R. DAS AMEAS · R. DE ALLER ULLOA · R.DAS ORFAS · FONTE DE SANTO ANTONIO · RÚA DA VIRXE DA CERCA · RÚA DO HÓRREO · RÚA DA ENSINANZA · RÚA DAS TROMPAS · PEXIGO DE ARRIBA · RÚA DOS PITELOS · RÚA DO MEDIO

Monasterio de San Martiño Pinario **7**
Praza do Obradoiro **2**
Praza da Inmaculada
Catedral **1**
Museo de las peregrinaciones **5**
Praza de Fonseca
Praza da Quintana
Praza de Cervantes
Porta do Camiño
Centro Galego de Arte Moderno **6**
Praza do Toural **i**
i
3
4
Mercado de abastos
Praza de Galicia
Praza de Mazarelos
8

Eating

Finding a place to eat in Santiago is hardly a problem. The city is famous for its seafood and fish and the meals to which pilgrims often treat themselves on completing their journey tend to centre around these (see box on page 165). To name just a few of the quality restaurants there is Casa Marcelo (telephone 0034 981 558 580) at calle Hortas, 1, Toñi Vicente (telephone 0034 981 594 100) at calle Rosalía de Castro, 24, Casa Manolo (telephone 0034 981 582 950) at plaza Cervantes s/n (no number) and El Asesino (telephone 0034 981 581 568) at plaza Universidad, 16.

Sleeping

In addition to the hostels listed on page 161, the city has a broad range of alternative accommodation. Some choose to reward themselves with a night at the luxury *parador* (telephone 0034 981 582 200) in plaza del Obradoiro. For those with more modest budgets, try boarding houses such as Pensión da Estrela (telephone 0034 981 576 924) at plaza San Martiño, 5, Hostal Alameda (telephone 0034 981 588 100) at rúa San Clemente, 32, Hostal Pazo de Agra (telephone 0034 981 882 660) at calle Caldeirería, 37 and Hostal La Carballinesca (telephone 0034 981 586 261) at calle Patio de Madres, 14.

Plaza del Obradoiro

The great plaza del Obradoiro is rectangular in shape and has an outstanding building on each of its four sides. To the north-west stands the cathedral with its Baroque façade and stairway, to the south-west the Reyes Católicos *parador*, formerly a pilgrims' hospice, to the south-east the Pazo de Raxoi, currently the seat of the presidency of the Galician regional government and also that of the city council, and to the north-east the San Xerome building, now the rectory of the university.

Old town

The traveller can spend hours wandering through the old town of Compostela, enticed by the porticoed calles Vilar and Nova, rúa do Franco with its fish restaurants, the famous Azabachería and plaza de las Platerías, which is pedestrianised and very pleasant.

Foods on display in the market

Market

The market is housed in an enormous stone building standing between rúa das Ameas and rúa da Virxe on the ring road that runs round the old town on a lower level. Morning is the best time to visit, as it is in full flow and is a hive of activity. In the afternoons and evenings only its souvenir stalls, bars and restaurants are open.

Pilgrimage museum

Rúa do Franco, bustling with life at all hours

This little museum, hidden away in calle San Miguel, houses some valuable works of art and provides the visitor

with explanations of the meaning that religious pilgrimages have for the different cultures of the world and the places where they have traditionally been undertaken.

Images from the Pilgrimage Museum and of Saint James

Galician Centre of Contemporary Art

The Portuguese architect Álvaro Siza designed this outwardly austere building, with flat walls and few apertures, close to the old monastery of Santo Domingo de Bonaval (Saint Dominic of Bonaval) on the edge of the old town.

Monastery of San Martiño Pinario (Saint Martin Pinario)

This centre of monastic power, where an atmosphere of great sobriety prevails, dates from the beginning of the tenth century and is now a seminary. The reredos of the main altar is its most admired feature. The ceilings and the Baroque sculptures are also outstanding.

Carballeira de Santa Susana

On ascending rúa San Clemente the traveller comes to an area of parkland known as La Alameda, part of which goes by the name of Carballeira de Santa Susana. It is a hill looking out over the old town. According to the locals, it is from here that you have the best of all views of the twin towers of the cathedral. It takes only a few minutes to walk up to and so escape briefly from the continuous bustle of the town.

The 'reward' of the seafood platter

There are practices which rapidly acquire the status of 'tradition' simply because they are so pleasurable. Among today's pilgrims, one such tradition is that of celebrating the accomplishment of the journey with a platter of seafood, to the extent that in the preceding days conversation tends to revolve largely around the arrangements for that celebration. In rúa do Franco, particularly, there are restaurants which serve seafood dishes at reasonable prices.

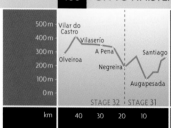

| 31 From Santiago de Compostela to Negreira |
| 32 From Negreira to Olveiroa |

31 19 km • 5 h
32 27.2 km • 7 h 10 min

→ **STAGE 31**

Santiago – Sarela de Baixo
35 min

The route out of Santiago takes you along rúa das Hortas, Poza de Bar, rúa San Lorenzo and Robleda de San Lorenzo. Then the yellow arrows guide you to a wooded area called Ponte Sarela. From there to Sarela de Baixo you walk on soft ground under a canopy of scented eucalyptuses on what is the pleasantest stretch of the day.

Sarela de Baixo – Alto de Vento
1 h 55 min

The path runs gently up and down from Sarela de Baixo to the village of Carballal, where you come to the ascent to the pass of Alto de Vento.

Alto de Vento – Augapesada
2 h 30 min

This section begins with a long descent on tarmac, although you soon have the benefit of a sort of pavement bordering the road.

Pazo de Cotón at Negreira

Augapesada – Alto do Mar de Ovellas
3 h 5 min

On leaving Augapesada you come to a climb which is gentle at first but becomes progressively steeper. When you reach a fountain you are barely a hundred metres from the top. The pass is not marked, but you reach the top when you come out onto a larger road.

Alto do Mar de Ovellas – Ponte Maceira
3 h 50 min

A gentle descent to the pretty town of Ponte Maceira.

Ponte Maceira – Negreira
5 h

This is a well-marked section running along the Tambre valley which takes you through the town of Barca. On reaching Negreira you have to cross the town to find the hostel, which stands at the top of a rise.

Negreira | 1h10min | Ponte Maceira | 1h20min | Augapesada | 1h25min | Carballal | 1h5min | **Santiago** ←

Olveiroa | 1h10min | Abeleiroas | 2h50min | Cornado | 2h5min | A Pena | 1h5min | **Negreira** ←

→ **STAGE 32**

Negreira – Zas
40 min

From the hostel in Negreira you return to the Way via a link that leads to the road. You then walk on to Zas through a eucalyptus wood.

Zas – A Pena
1 h 5 min

Having now left the wood behind, you will now be without shade almost right up to the end of the stage.

A Pena – Vilaserío
2 h 45 min

Once past the village of Portocamiño you come out onto the road and then walk on tarmac to Vilaserío.

Vilaserío – Cornado
3 h 10 min

After Vilaserío you have to cross the road to enter Cornado. You then leave the tarmac and return to a comfortable woodland track.

Cornado – Maroñas
4 h 15 min

The land rises and falls but is not too difficult. From time to time you have to cross a road, but the route is well marked throughout. A descent takes you to Maroñas.

Maroñas – Abeleiroas
6 h

On this section we find a lot of tarmac as a result of the closure of a track leading to Monte Aro. Apparently this was caused by the landowner.

Abeleiroas – Olveiroa
7 h 10 min

Still on tarmac and heading, in general, downward, you cross the river Xallas and enter Olveiroa. The hostel there has a number of buildings.

The hostel at Olveiroa, pleasant in appearance and perfectly equipped

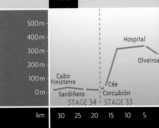

33 From Olveiroa
to Corcubión

34 From Corcubión
to Finisterre

km	30	25	20	15	10	5

33 18.4 km • 4 h 45 min
34 15.6 km • 4 h 15 min

→ **STAGE 33**
Olveiroa – Hospital
1 h 15 min

Returning to the road, turn off to the left almost immediately. The turning is marked, but it is easy to miss if you're not careful. You then come to a track which leads quite steeply upward and takes you close to the wind turbines. Cross a concrete bridge and so come to the village of Hospital.

Hospital – Crucero Marco do Couto
1 h 55 min

Go past the bar and up the road until you come to twin marker stones where a turning to Muxia is indicated. Follow the sign to Fisterra. From this point practically all the rest of the stage is downhill, with just the occasional short ascent.

Crucero Marco do Couto – Nose

Señora das Neves
2 h 20 min

The stone cross of Marco do Couto stands on a kind of small plateau thick with scrub. Turn to the left, thus coming into line with the road, and then again to the right to descend towards the chapel of Nose Señora das Neves (Our Lady of the Snows). This has a visitor's book and a collection of votive offerings left by the faithful and by pilgrims.

Nose Señora das Neves – Alto Cruceiro da Armada
3 h 35 min

Here the path leads upward. Just before reaching the cross you have your first glimpse of the Atlantic Ocean.

Alto Cruceiro da Armada – Cée
4 h 30 min

A very sharp downhill stretch takes you to the pretty town of Cée.

Cée – Corcubión
4 h 45 min

To go from Cée to Corcubión you only have to cross the bay, but that entails a rather stiff ascent.

The promenade at Cée, at the end of the town

| Corcubión | 15 h | Cée | 2 h 10 min | Nosa Señoras das Neves | 1 h 5 min | Hospital | 1 h 15 min | **Olveiroa** |
| **Finisterre** | 1 h 20 min | Fisterra | 1 h 30 min | Sardiñeiro | 1 h 25 min | **Corcubión** |

The lighthouse (km 0) and the tribute to the pilgrim

→ STAGE 34
Corcubión – Sardiñeiro
1 h 25 min

This stage may look very short on the map, but bear in mind that although it ends at the lighthouse of Finisterre you will have to walk back to Fisterra afterwards. That adds almost an hour and a half to the total journey time, unless you are fortunate enough to hitch a lift on the return.

On this section the route has alternate stretches of road and woodland and scented pines provide shade. It runs parallel to the coast throughout and has, as a result, some steep inclines.

Sardiñeiro – Fisterra
2 h 55 min

The trend remains the same. At times you walk along the shoulder of the road. At others the path takes you past splendid, unspoilt beaches. As this is the final stage and there are only a few hours still ahead, you may well be tempted to have a swim if the weather is right.

On arriving at Fisterra the best plan is to reserve a bed at the hostel and leave your backpack there, so you can go on to the cape carrying nothing more than a camera.

Fisterra – Finisterre
4 h 15 min

The stretch between Fisterra and the cape is unpleasant. It is road all the way and the shoulder is at best very narrow and at worst non-existent. The reward, however, is that you come to the end of the world, the Finis Terrae of the Romans.

After passing the lighthouse you come to a humble but fitting tribute to the pilgrim: a monument in the form of a boot worked in metal (there were two, but one has disappeared). You will also see the hole where some travellers perform the symbolic ritual of burning their clothes.

LIST OF **HOSTELS**

N.B. The details given below are based on information provided by the hostels themselves. Opening dates may change. In the event of doubt or when the journey is being undertaken outside the summer months, the best course is to telephone beforehand in order to check.

STAGE 1
Saint Jean-Pied-de-Port (Donibane Garazi)
• Gite d'etape L'Esprit du Chemin.
Rue de la Citadelle, 40.
Tel. 0033 559 372 468. 18 beds.
www.espritduchemin.org.
Open from April to September.
8€ per night. Closing hour: 22.00h
• Gite d'etape Le Chemin vers l'Étoile.
Rue d'Espagne, 21.
Tel. 0033 559 372 071. 20 beds. Open all year.
8€ per night. Closing hour: 22.00h
• Albergue Ultreia.
Rue de la Citadelle, 8.
Tel. 0033 680 884 622. 15 beds.
Open from April to October.
From 12 to 15€ per night. Closing hour: 22.00h
• Refugio Accueil Pelerin.
Rue de la Citadelle, 55.
Tel. 0033 559 370 509. 24 beds.
Open from March to November.
8€ with breakfast. Closing hour: 22.00h
• Albergue Ferme Ithurburia.
Honto (St Michel).
Tel. 0033 559 371 117. 22 beds. Open all year.
14€ per night. No closing hour.

Orisson
• Refugio de montaña. On the Way.
Tel. 0033 559 491 303. 18 beds.
www.refuge-orisson.com
Open from April to September.
31€ half-board. Closing hour: 21.30h

Luzaide – Valcarlos
• Albergue municipal. Pza. Santiago.
Tel. 0034 646 048 883. 24 beds. Open all year.
10€ with breakfast. No closing hour.

Orreaga – Roncesvalles
• Albergue Itzandegia.
Former pilgrims' hospice.
Tel. 0034 948 760 000. 118 beds at hostel +
120 in bungalows. Open all year. 6€ per night.
Closing hour: 22.00h

STAGE 2
Zubiri
• Albergue municipal. Old schoolhouses.
Tel. 0034 628 324 186. 52 beds.
Open from March to 15 October.
6€ per night. Closing hour: 22.00h

• Albergue Zaldiko. C/. Puente de la Raba, 1.
Tel. 0034 609 736 420. 24 beds.
www.alberguezaldiko.com.
Open from March to October.
10€ per night. No closing hour.
(Warn the *hospitalera* if late arrival is
anticipated.)
• Albergue el Palo de Avellano.
Avenida de Roncesvalles, 16.
Tel. 0034 948 304 770. 57 beds.
Open from March to November.
May accept reservations rest of year.
15€ with breakfast. Closing hour: 22.00h

Larrasoaña
• Albergue municipal.
Tel. 0034 605 505 489. 58 beds.
Open all year except for Christmas holidays.
6€ per night. No closing hour.

STAGE 3
Trinidad de Arre
• Albergue de la Trinidad de Arre. Av. Zubiri.
Tel. 0034 948 332 941. 34 beds.
Open from 16 February to 15 December.
7€ per night. Closing hour: 22.00h

Villava
• Albergue municipal.
C/. Pedro de Atarrabia, 17–19,
trasera, Villava (a town some 5 km
from Pamplona).
Tel. 0034 948 581 804. 48 beds.
Open all year except Christmas.
12.40€ per night. Closing hour: 23.00h

Huarte
• Albergue municipal. Plaza San Juan s/n
(a town some 8 km from Pamplona).
Tel. 0034 948 074 329. 60 beds.
Open from April to September.
10€ per night. Closing hour: 22.00h

Pamplona (Iruña)
• Albergue de Jesús y María.
C/. Compañía, 4.
Tel. 0034 948 222 644. 114 beds.
Open all year except the week of
San Fermín (from 6 July) and Christmas.
6€ per night. Closing hour: 23.00h

• Albergue Casa Paderborn.
C/. Playa de Caparroso, 6.
Tel. 0034 948 211 712. 26 beds.
Open from March to October.
6€ per night. Closing hour: 22.00h

STAGE 4
Cizur Menor
• Albergue Cizur Menor.
Encomienda Sanjuanista.
Tel. 0034 616 651 330. 28 beds.
Open from May to September.
4€ per night. Closing hour: 21.30h
• Albergue Familia Roncal.
Pº Lurbeltzeta.
Tel. 0034 948 183 885. 51 beds.
Open all year except November.
www.elalberguedemaribel.com.
8€ per night. Closing hour: 22.00h

Zariquiegui
• El Albergue de Zariquiegui.
C/. San Andrés, 16.
Tel. 0034 948 353 353. 16 beds.
Open from Holy Week to early December.
10€ with breakfast. Closing hour: 22.00h

Uterga
• Albergue Camino del Perdón.
C/. Mayor, 57.
Tel. 0034 948 344 598. 16 beds.
www.caminodelperdon.es.
Open from March to November.
10€ per night. Closing hour: 21.30h

Óbanos
• Albergue Usda.
C/. San Lorenzo, 6.
Tel. 0034 676 560 927. 36 beds.
Open from April to October.
7€ per night. Closing hour: 22.00h

Puente la Reina (Gares)
• Albergue de los Padres Reparadores.
C/. Crucifijo, 1.
Tel. 0034 948 340 050. 100 beds.
Open all year.
4€ per night. Closing hour: 23.00h
• Albergue Jakue. C/. Irunbidea s/n.
Tel. 0034 948 341 017. 92 beds.
Open from March to October.
www. jakue.com.
9€ per night. Closing hour: 23.00h
• Albergue Santiago Apóstol. Paraje El Real.
Tel. 0034 948 340 220. 100 beds.
Open from April to October.
8€ per night. Closing hour: 23.00h

STAGE 5
Mañeru
• Albergue de Peregrinos Lurgorri.
C/. Esperanza, 5, bajo.
Tel. 0034 649 021 705. 12 beds.
Open from April to October.
10€ per night with breakfast.
Closing hour: 22.00h

Cirauqui
• Albergue Maralotx.
C/. San Román, 30.
Tel. 0034 678 635 208. 32 beds.
Open from March to October.
10€ per night. Closing hour: 22.00h

Lorca
• Albergue de Lorca. C/. Mayor, 40.
Tel. 0034 948 541 190. 14 beds.
Open from April to October.
7€ per night. Closing hour: 22.00h
• Albergue La Bodega del Camino.
C/. Placeta, 8.
Tel. 0034 948 541 162. 36 beds.
www.labodegadelcamino.com.
Open all year but, from November to March,
only for groups with prior reservation.
8€ per night. No closing hour

Villatuerta
• Albergue de Vilatuerta. C/. Rebote, 5.
Tel. 0034 948 536 095. 40 beds.
www.alberguevillatuerta.com.
Open from Holy Week to November.
10€ per night. Closing hour: 22.00h

Estella (Lizarra)
• Hospital de Peregrinos. C/. La Rúa, 50.
Tel. 0034 948 550 200. 100 beds. Open all year
except for Christmas holidays.
7€ with breakfast. Closing hour: 22.00h
• Albergue San Miguel.
C/. Mercado Viejo, 18.
Tel. 0034 948 550 431. 36 beds. Open all year.
Relies on voluntary donations.
Closing hour: 22.00h
• Albergue de Anfas. C/. Cordeleros, 7.
Tel. 0034 680 459 798. 34 beds.
Open from May to September.
6€ per night. Closing hour: 22.00h

Ayegui
• Albergue municipal. Polideportivo.
Tel. 0034 948 554 311. 70 beds.
Open all year.
6€ per night. Closing hour: 22.00h
• Albergue San Cipriano de Ayegui.
C/. Polideportivo, 3.
Tel. 0034 948 554 311. 80 beds. Open all year.
6€ per night. Closing hour: 22.00h

STAGE 6
Irache
• **Albergue juvenil Oncineda.**
C/. Monasterio de Irache s/n.
Tel. 0034 948 555 022. 150 beds.
Open from April to November.
9€ per night. Closing hour: 22.00h

Villamayor de Monjardín
• **Albergue Santa Cruz.** C/. Santa María.
No telephone. 25 beds.
Open from April to October.
Relies on voluntary donations.
Closing hour: 22.00h
• **Albergue Hogar Monjardín.**
Plaza de la Iglesia.
Tel. 0034 948 537 136. 25 beds.
Open from April to November.
5€ per night. Closing hour: 23.00h

Los Arcos
• **Albergue Isaac Santiago.**
C/. San Lázaro s/n.
Tel. 0034 948 441 091. 70 beds.
Open from April to October.
4€ per night. Closing hour: 22.00h
• **Albergue de la Fuente Casa de Austria.**
Travesía del Estanco, 5.
Tel. 0034 948 640 797. 54 beds.
Open all year except January.
8€ per night. Closing hour: 22.30h
• **Albergue Casa Alberdi.** C/. Hortal, 3.
Tel. 0034 948 640 764. 30 beds. Open all year.
7€ per night. Closing hour: 23.00h
• **Albergue Casa de la Abuela.**
Plaza de la Fruta, 8.
Tel. 0034 948 640 250. 38 beds.
Open from March to October.
Outside those months reservations may
be made by telephone.
8€ per night. Closing hour: 22.00h

Sansol
• **Albergue Arcadi y Nines.** C/. Taconera, 10.
Tel. 0034 618 197 520. 14 beds.
Open from April to October.
4€ per night. Closing hour: 22.30h

Torres del Río
• **Albergue Casa Mari.** C/. Casas Nuevas, 13.
Tel. 0034 948 648 409. 26 beds. Open all year.
7€ per night. Closing hour: 22.30h
• **Albergue Casa Mariela.**
Pza. Valeriano Ordóñez, 6.
Tel. 0034 948 648 251. 54 beds. Open all year.
7€ per night. Closing hour: 22.00h
• **Albergue La Pata de Oca.** C/Mayor, 5.
Tel. 0034 948 378 457. 84 beds. Open all year.
10€ per night. Closing hour: 00.00h

STAGE 7
Viana
• **Albergueria Andrés Muñoz.**
C/. Ruina de San Pedro s/n.
Tel. 0034 948 645 530. 54 beds.
Open from March to October.
Outside those months reservations are
taken at Tel. 0034 609 141 798.
6€ per night. Closing hour: 22.00h
• **Albergue parroquial.** Pza. Fueros.
Tel. 0034 948 645 037. 15 beds.
Open from mid-June to September.
Relies on voluntary donations.
Closing hour: 22.00h

Logroño
• **Albergue de peregrinos de Logroño.**
C/. Rúavieja, 32.
Tel. 0034 941 248 686. 68 beds.
Open from March to October.
7€ per night. Closing hour: 22.00h
• **Albergue Puerta del Revellín.**
Pza. Martínez Flamarique, 4.
Tel. 0034 941 700 832. 40 beds. Open all year.
10.50€ per night. Closing hour: 22.30h
• **Albergue parroquial de Santiago.**
C/ Barriocepo, 8, 1º.
No telephone. 30 beds.
Open from June to September.
Relies on voluntary donations.
Communal dinner. No closing hour.

STAGE 8
Navarrete
• **Albergue de Navarrete.**
C/. San Juan s/n.
Tel. 0034 941 440 776. 50 beds.
Open from March to November.
Reservations accepted by telephone for
groups in rest of year.
5€ per night. Closing hour: 22.00h
• **Albergue El Cántaro.** C/. Herrerías, 16.
Tel. 0034 941 441 180. 31 beds. Open all year.
10€ per night. Closing hour: 23.00h

Sotés
• **Albergue Bodega Fernando J. Rodríguez.**
C/ Conde de Garay, 25.
Tel. 0034 670 053 229. 18 beds.
Open from late April to October.
15€ with breakfast. No closing hour.

Ventosa
• **Albergue San Saturnino.**
C/. Medio derecha, 9.
Tel. 0034 941 441 899. 42 beds. Open all year.
8€ per night. Closing hour: 22.00h

Nájera
• Albergue de peregrinos de Nájera.
Pza. Santiago.
No telephone. 92 beds.
Open all year.
Relies on voluntary donations.
Closing hour: 22.00h
• Albergue Sancho III. C/. San Marcial, 6.
Tel. 0034 941 361 138. 10 beds.
Open from Holy Week to October.
8€ per night. Closing hour: 22.00h

STAGE 9
Azofra
• Albergue de peregrinos de Azofra.
C/. Las Parras, 7.
Tel. 0034 941 379 049. 60 beds. Open all year.
6€ per night. Closing hour: 22.00h

Cirueña
• Albergue Virgen de Guadalupe.
Calle Barrio Alto, 1.
Tel. 0034 638 924 069. 14 beds.
Open from 15 March to 15 October.
10€ per night. Closing hour: 22.00h
• Albergue Virgen de las Candelas.
Calle Real, 90.
Tel. 0034 941 343 290. 22 beds. Open all year.
8€ per night. Closing hour: 22.00h

Santo Domingo de la Calzada
• Casa del Santo. C/. Mayor, 38.
Tel. 0034 941 343 390. 210 beds. Open all year.
Relies on voluntary donations.
Closing hour: 22.00h
• Albergue de la Abadía Cisterciense.
C/. Mayor, 29.
Tel. 0034 941 340 570. 33 beds.
Open from June to September.
5€ per night. Closing hour: 22.00h

STAGE 10
Grañón
• Albergue San Juan Bautista.
Beside the church.
No telephone. 40 beds. Open all year.
Relies on voluntary donations. No closing hour.
• Albergue juvenil Carrasquedo.
Outside the town.
Tel. 0034 941 746 000. 40 beds. Open all year.
For those under 30:
10.30€ per night + 1.50€ cleaning costs
For those 30 and over:
12.36€ per night + 1.50€ cleaning costs
Closing hour: 21.00h

Redecilla del Camino
• Albergue municipal San Lázaro.
C/. Mayor, 24.
Tel. 0034 947 580 283. 38 beds. Open all year.
Relies on voluntary donations. No closing hour.

Viloria
• Refugio de peregrinos Acacio y Orienta.
C/. Nueva, 6.
Tel. 0034 947 585 220. 10 beds.
Open from March to October.
5€ per night; breakfast and dinner
on voluntary donation basis.
Closing hour: 22.00h

Villamayor del Río
• Albergue San Luis de Francia.
Ctra. de Quintanilla s/n.
Tel. 0034 947 580 566. 26 beds. Open all year.
5€ per night. Closing hour: 22.00h

Belorado
• Albergue A Santiago.
Camino Redoña s/n.
Tel. 0034 677 811 847. 98 beds. Open all year.
5€ per night. Closing hour: 23.00h
• Refugio parroquial de Belorado.
Bº El Corro s/n.
Tel. 0034 947 580 085. 24 beds.
Open from May to November.
Relies on voluntary donations.
Closing hour: 22.00h.
• Albergue de peregrinos Caminante.
C/. Mayor, 36.
Tel. 0034 656 873 927. 26 beds.
Open from March to October.
5€ per night. Closing hour: 22.00h
• Albergue El Corro. C/. Mayor, 68.
Tel. 0034 670 691 173. 45 beds. Open all year.
13.50€ with breakfast. No closing hour.
• Albergue Cuatro Cantones.
C/. López Bernal, 10.
Tel. 0034 696 427 707. 60 beds. Open all year.
5€ per night. Closing hour: 22.00h

STAGE 11
Tosantos
• Albergue San Francisco de Asís.
C/. Santa Marina.
Tel. 0034 947 580 085. 30 beds.
Open from March to November.
Relies on voluntary donations.
Closing hour: 22.00h

Villambistia
• Albergue San Roque. Plaza Mayor.
Tel. 0034 660 797 011. 14 beds.
Open all year except for the last week of
January and of February. Closed every Tuesday.
5€ per night. Closing hour: 23.00h

Espinosa del Camino
• Albergue La Campana.
Espinosa s/n.
Tel. 0034 678 479 361. 10 beds.
Open all year except for Christmas holidays.
5€ per night. Closing hour: 22.00h

Villafranca de Montes de Oca
• **Albergue de Villafranca.** C/. Mayor s/n.
Tel. 0034 947 582 124. 60 beds. Open all year.
6€ per night. Closing hour: 22.30h
• **Albergue San Antón Abad.** C/ Hospital, 4
(beside the old pilgrims' hospice).
Tel. 0034 947 582 150. 30 beds.
Open from March to 15 November.
8€ per night. Closing hour: 00.00h

San Juan de Ortega
• **Albergue de San Juan de Ortega.**
Tel. 0034 947 560 438. 60 beds.
Open from March to November.
5€ per night. Closing hour: 22.00h

Agés
• **Albergue San Rafael.**
Camino San Juan de Ortega, s/n
Tel. 0034 947 430 392. 16 beds.
www.activeb.es/alberguesanrafael2010/
index.html
Open all year.
10€ per night. Closing hour: 22.00h
• **Albergue El Pajar de Agés.**
C/. Paralela del Medio, 12.
Tel. 0034 947 400 629. 34 beds.
Open from March to October.
8€ per night. Closing hour: 22.00h.
• **Albergue municipal de Agés.**
C/. del Medio, 21.
Tel. 0034 947 400 697. 36 beds. Open all year.
8€ per night. Closing hour: 23.30h

STAGE 12
Atapuerca
• **Albergue La Hutte.** C/. Enmedio, 36.
Tel. 0034 947 430 320. 18 beds. Open all year.
5€ per night. Closing hour: 22.30h.
• **Centro turístico El Peregrino.**
C/. Carretera, 105.
Tel. 0034 661 580 882. 36 beds.
Open from March to November.
8€ per night. Closing hour: 22.00h

Olmos de Atapuerca
• **Albergue de Olmos de Atapuerca.**
C/. Iglesia.
Tel. 0034 947 430 444. 24 beds.
Open all year except February.
7€ per night. No closing hour.

Burgos
• **Albergue municipal.** C/. Fernán González, 28.
Tel. 0034 947 460 922. 150 beds. Open all year.
4€ per night. Closing hour: 22.30h
• **Albergue Santiago y Santa Catalina.**
C/. Laín Calvo, 10.
Tel. 0034 947 207 952. 16 beds.
Open from March to November.
Relies on voluntary donations.
Closing hour: 22.30h

• **Casa de Peregrinos Emaús.**
C/. San Pedro de Cardeña.
No telephone. 20 beds.
Open from April to November.
Relies on voluntary donations.
Closing hour: 20.00h
• **Albergue Divina Pastora.** C/. Lain Calvo, 10.
Tel. 0034 947 207 952. 16 beds.
Open from Holy Week to mid-October.
Relies on voluntary donations.
Closing hour: 21.00h

STAGE 13
Tardajos
• **Albergue de Tardajos.** C/. Asunción s/n.
Tel. 0034 947 451 189. 18 beds. Open all year.
Relies on voluntary donations.
Closing hour: 22.00h

Rabé de las Calzadas
• **Hospital Santa Marina y Santiago.**
Pza. Ribera, 6.
Tel. 0034 607 664 122. 8 beds.
Open from April to November.
8€ per night. Closing hour: 22.00h
• **Albergue Liberanos domine.** Pza. Ribera, 2.
Tel. 0034 695 116 901. 24 beds. Open all year.
8€ per night. Closing hour: 22.00h

Hornillos del Camino
• **Albergue de Hornillos.** Pza. Iglesia.
Tel. 0034 947 471 220. 32 beds.
Open all year except February.
6€ per night. Closing hour: 22.00h

Arroyo San Bol
• **Albergue Arroyo de San Bol.**
Tel. 0034 696 858 770. 12 beds.
Open from March to October.
5€ including dinner. No closing hour.

Hontanas
• **Albergue de Hontanas.** C/. Real, 26.
Tel. 0034 947 377 021. 55 beds. Open all year.
5€ per night. No closing hour.
• **Mesón-albergue El Puntido.** C/. Iglesia, 6.
Tel. 0034 947 378 597. 54 beds.
Open from Holy Week to October.
5€ per night. Closing hour: 21.30h
• **Albergue Santa Brígida.** C/ Real, 15.
Tel. 0034 628 927 317. 14 beds.
Open from 12 March to late October.
6€ per night. No closing hour.

STAGE 14
San Antón
• **Hospital de peregrinos de San Antón.**
Convento de San Antón,
3.6 km before Castrojeriz.
No telephone. 12 beds.
Open from May to September.
Relies on voluntary donations.
Closing hour: 20.00h

Castrojeriz
• **Refugio tradicional de Castrojeriz.**
C/. Cordón.
Tel. 0034 947 377 400. 28 beds.
Open from April to October.
Relies on voluntary donations.
Closing hour: 22.30h
• **Albergue de Castrojeriz.**
C/. Virgen del Manzano s/n.
Tel. 0034 947 377 255. 35 beds.
Open from March to November.
6€ per night. No closing hour.
• **Albergue Casa Nostra.**
C/. Real de Oriente, 54.
Tel. 0034 947 377 493. 26 beds.
Open from late February to early December.
6.50€ per night. Closing hour: 22.00h
• **Albergue de San Esteban.**
Beside Plaza Mayor.
Tel. 0034 947 377 001. 30 beds. Open all year.
Relies on voluntary donations.
Closing hour: 22.30h

Itero del Castillo
• **Albergue de Itero del Castillo.**
Pza. Ayuntamiento.
Tel. 0034 608 977 477. 7 beds.
Open all year.
5€ per night. No closing hour.

Ermita de San Nicolás
• **Albergue de San Nicolás.**
No telephone. 12 beds.
Open from June to September.
Relies on voluntary donations.
Closes at nightfall.

Itero de la Vega
• **Albergue municipal.** Pza. Iglesia.
No telephone. 20 beds. Open all year.
3€ per night. Closing hour: 22.30h
• **Albergue de Itero.** C/. Santa Ana, 3.
Tel. 0034 979 151 781. 18 beds. Open all year.
5€ per night. Closing hour: 22.00h
• **Albergue Puente Fitero.** C/. Santa María, 3.
Tel. 0034 979 151 822. 20 beds. Open all year.
6€ per night. Closing hour: 22.00h

Boadilla del Camino
• **Albergue de Boadilla del Camino.**
C/. Escuelas.
Tel. 0034 979 810 390. 12 beds. Open all year.
3€ per night. Closing hour: 22.00h
• **Albergue En el Camino.** Pza. Rollo.
Tel. 0034 979 810 284. 48 beds.
Open from March to early November.
6€ per night. Closing hour: 22.00h
• **Albergue Putzu.** C/. Bodegas, 9.
inconformista@hotmail.com
No telephone. 16 beds.
Open all year except for Christmas holidays.
7€ per night. Closes at nightfall.

STAGE 15
Frómista
• **Albergue de Frómista.** Pza. San Martín.
Tel. 0034 979 811 089. 56 beds.
Open all year except Christmas and January.
7€ per night. Closing hour: 23.00h
• **Albergue Estrella del Camino.**
Av. Ejército español.
Tel. 0034 979 810 053. 34 beds.
Open from March to November. Available
rest of year for groups of over 20 people.
7€ per night. Closing hour: 23.00h
• **Albergue Canal de Castilla.**
C/ La Estación, s/n. At the entrance to the
town, after the railway underpass.
Tel. 0034 979 810 193. 40 beds.
Open from April to November.
7€ per night. Closing hour: 22.00h

Población de Campos
• **Albergue de Población de Campos.**
Pº Cementerio.
Tel. 0034 979 811 099. 18 beds. Open all year.
4/5€ per night. No closing hour.

Villarmentero de Campos
• **Albergue de Villarmentero de Campos.** C/.
José Antonio, 2.
Tel. 0034 629 178 543. 40 beds.
Open from April to October.
6€ per night. No closing hour.

Villalcázar de Sirga
• **Albergue Villalcázar de Sirga.**
Tel. 0034 979 888 041. 20 beds.
Open from April to October.
Relies on voluntary donations.
Closing hour: 23.00h
• **Albergue Tasca Don Camilo.**
No telephone. 26 beds. Open all year.
7€ per night. Closing hour: 22.00h

Carrión de los Condes
• **Albergue Espíritu Santo.** Pza. San Juan, 4.
Tel. 0034 979 880 052. 90 beds. Open all year.
5€ per night. Closing hour: 22.00h
• **Albergue Santa María.** Beside the church.
Tel. 0034 979 880 768. 52 beds.
Open from March to October.
5€ per night. Closing hour: 22.00h
• **Monasterio de Santa Clara.**
C/. Santa Clara, 1.
Tel. 0034 979 880 837. 31 beds.
Open from March to November.
5€ per night. Closing hour: 23.00h
• **Albergue juvenil Río Carrión.**
Pza. Champagnat, 1.
Tel. 0034 979 881 063. 300 beds. Open all year
but only for groups of over 50 people.
12€ per night. Closing hour: 00.00h

STAGE 16
Villada (a diversion in Calzadilla)
• **Albergue Jacobeo Julián Campo y José Santino Manzano.**
Calle Ferial Nuevo, s/n.
Tel. 0034 979 844 005. 20 beds. Open all year.
5€ per night. No closing hour.

Calzadilla de la Cueza
• **Albergue de Calzadilla.**
Tel. 0034 979 883 187. 80 beds. Open all year.
7€ per night. No closing hour.

Lédigos
• **Albergue El Palomar.** C/. Ronda de Abajo.
Tel. 0034 979 883 605. 52 beds.
Open all year except December and January.
6€ per night. Closing hour: 23.00h

Terradillos de Templarios
• **Albergue Jacques de Molay.** C/. Iglesia.
Tel. 0034 979 883 679. 49 beds.
Open all year except for Christmas holidays.
7€ per night. Closing hour: 23.00h
• **Albergue Los Templarios.**
Tel. 0034 667 252 279. 52 beds.
Open from March to October.
www.alberguelostemplarios.com.
7€ per night. Closing hour: 22.30h

STAGE 17
San Nicolás del Real Camino
• **Alberguería Laganares.** Pza. Iglesia.
Tel. 0034 979 188 142. 22 beds.
Open from March to November.
7€ per night. Closing hour: 22.00h

Sahagún
• **Albergue de peregrinos Cluny.**
Iglesia de la Trinidad.
Tel. 0034 987 782 117. 64 beds. Open all year.
4€ per night. Closing hour: 22.00h
• **Albergue de las Madres Benedictinas.**
Closed for works at time of writing
• **Albergue Viatoris.** C/. Arco Travesía, 25.
Tel. 0034 987 780 975. 50 beds.
www.viatoris.es. Open from March to October.
7€ per night. Closing hour: 22.30h

Calzada del Coto
• **Albergue de Calzada del Coto.** C/. Real s/n.
Tel. 0034 987 781 233. 24 beds. Open all year.
Relies on voluntary donations.
No closing hour.

Bercianos del Real Camino
• **Albergue Bercianos.** C/. Santa Rita, 11.
Tel. 0034 987 784 008. 46 beds.
Open from April to November.
Relies on voluntary donations.
No closing hour.

El Burgo Ranero
• **Albergue de Calzadilla de los Hermanillos.**
Tel. 0034 987 330 023. 22 beds. Open all year.
Relies on voluntary donations.
Closing hour: 22.00h
• **Albergue Domenico Laffi.** Pza. Mayor.
Tel. 0034 987 330 047. 28 beds. Open all year.
Relies on voluntary donations.
Closing hour: 22.00h
• **Albergue La Laguna.**
C/. Laguna, 12.
Tel. 0034 987 330 094. 18 beds.
Open from Holy Week to November.
8€ per night. Closing hour: 23.00h
• **Albergue El Nogal.**
C/. Fray Pedro, 42.
Tel. 0034 627 229 331. 30 beds.
Open from Holy Week to November.
7€ per night. Closing hour: 22.30h
• **Albergue Ebalo Tamaú.** C/ La Estación, 37.
Tel. 0034 679 490 521. 12 beds.
Open from early April to mid-October.
8€ per night. Closing hour: 00.00h

STAGE 18
Reliegos
• **Albergue de Reliegos.**
C/. Escuela.
Tel. 0034 987 317 801. 45 beds. Open all year.
5€ per night. Closing hour: 23.00h

Mansilla de las Mulas
• **Albergue de Mansilla de las Mulas.**
C/. Puente, 5.
Tel. 0034 661 977 305. 76 beds.
Open all year except December.
5€ per night. Closing hour: 23.00h
• **Albergue El Jardín del Camino.**
C/ Camino de Santiago, 1.
Tel. 0034 987 310 232. 32 beds.
Open all year except Christmas.
From 8 to 10€. Closes from 22.00 to 23.00h

Puente Villarente
• **Albergue San Pelayo.** C/. Romero, 9.
Tel. 0034 650 918 281. 56 beds. Open all year.
8€ per night. Closing hour: 22.00h

Arcahueja
• **Albergue La Torre.** C/. Torre, 1.
Tel. 0034 669 660 914. 22 beds.
Open all year except for Christmas holidays and February.
7–8€ per night. Closing hour: 22.00h

STAGE 19
León
• **Albergue Ciudad de León.**
C/. Campos Góticos s/n.
Tel. 0034 987 081 832. 64 beds.
Open all year except Christmas.
5€ per night. No closing hour.

• Albergue Santa María de Carvajal.
Pza. Santa María del Camino.
Tel. 0034 987 252 866. 142 beds.
Open from February to December.
Relies on voluntary donations.
Closing hour: 21.30h

La Virgen del Camino
• Albergue don Antonino y doña Cinia.
Camino de Villacedré, 16.
Tel. 0034 987 302 213. 40 beds.
Open from April to October.
5€ per night. Closing hour: 23.00h

Valverde de la Virgen
• La Casa del Camino. Camino El Jano, 2.
Tel. 0034 659 178 087. 20 beds. Open all year.
8€ per night. No closing hour.

Villadangos del Páramo
• Albergue de Villadangos del Páramo.
Carretera a Villadangos del Páramo.
Tel. 0034 987 390 003. 85 beds. Open all year.
3€ per night. Closing hour: 22.45h

Villar de Mazarife (turn-off after Virgen del Camino)
• Albergue San Antonio de Padua.
C/. León, 33.
Tel. 0034 987 390 192. 60 beds. Open all year.
6€ per night. Closing hour: 22.00h
• Albergue Casa de Jesús. C/. Corujo, 11.
Tel. 0034 987 390 697. 50 beds. Open all year.
5€ per night. Closing hour: 23.00h
• Albergue Casa Pepe. C/. Teso, 2.
Tel. 0034 987 390 517. 26 beds.
Open from March to December.
7€ per night. Closing hour: 23.00h

San Martín del Camino
• Albergue de San Martín del Camino.
Carretera de León – Astorga.
Tel. 0034 634 467 629 (Luis). 60 beds.
Open all year.
3€ per night. Closing hour: 23.00h
• Albergue Santa Ana.
Ctra. de Astorga, 3.
Tel. 0034 987 378 653. 94 beds. Open all year.
4€ per night. No closing hour.
• Albergue Vieira.
Avenida Peregrinos s/n.
Tel. 0034 987 378 565. 60 beds.
Open from March to October.
From 3€ per night. Closing hour: 22.00h

STAGE 20
Hospital de Órbigo
• Refugio Hospital de Órbigo.
C/. Álvarez Vega, 32.
Tel. 0034 987 388 444. 90 beds.
Open from March to October.
5€ per night. Closing hour: 22.30h

• Albergue San Miguel. C/. Álvarez Vega, 35.
Tel. 0034 987 388 285. 40 beds.
Open from Holy Week to October.
7€ per night. Closing hour: 22.00h

Villares de Órbigo
• Albergue turístico de Villares de Órbigo.
Calle Arnal, 21.
Tel. 0034 987 132 935. 28 beds.
Open all year except Christmas holidays
and January.
6€ per night. Closing hour: 23.00h

Santibáñez de Valdeiglesias
• Albergue Santibáñez de Valdeiglesias.
C/. Caromonte bajo, 3.
Tel. 0034 987 377 698. 20 beds.
Open from March to October.
6€ per night. No closing hour.

Astorga
• Albergue San Javier. C/. Portería, 6.
Tel. 0034 987 618 532. 95 beds.
Open from March to November.
8€ per night. Closing hour: 22.30h
• Albergue Siervas de María.
Pza. San Francisco, 3.
Tel. 0034 987 616 034. 154 beds. Open all year.
5€ per night. Closing hour: 23.00h
• Albergue de Astorga.
Plaza de los Marqueses, 3
Tel. 0034 987 547 751. 195 beds.
Open from mid-March to September.
3€ per night. Closing hour: 23.00h
• Albergue Camino y Vía.
On the Way, before entering Astorga and
after the footbridge over the railway.
Tel. 0034 987 615 192. 22 beds.
Open from mid-February to mid-November.
6€ per night. No closing hour.

STAGE 21
Murias de Rechivaldo
• Albergue Murias de Rechivaldo.
Ctra. Santa Colomba.
Tel. 0034 987 691 150. 20 beds.
Open from April to October.
4€ per night. Closing hour: 22.30h
• Albergue Las Águedas.
C/. Camino de Santiago, 52.
Tel. 0034 987 691 234. 46 beds. Open from
March to November. Reservations only for
large groups accepted in winter months.
8€ per night. No closing hour.

Santa Catalina de Somoza
• Hospedería San Blas.
C/. Real, 11.
Tel. 0034 987 691 411. 24 beds.
www.hospederiasanblas.com. Open all year.
5€ per night. Closing hour: 23.00h

• **Albergue y centro de turismo rural El Caminante.**
C/. Real, 2. Tel. 0034 987 691 098.
www.elcaminante.es.
16 beds. Open all year.
6€ per night. No closing hour.

El Ganso
• **Albergue Gabino.** C/. Real.
Tel. 0034 660 912 823. 28 beds.
Open from Holy Week to early November.
8€ with breakfast. No closing hour.

Rabanal del Camino
• **Albergue municipal Rabanal del Camino.**
Pza. Morán Alonso. No telephone. 34 beds.
Open from April to October.
4€ per night. Closing hour: 22.30h
• **Albergue La Senda**
(formerly Albergue El Tesín).
C/. Real. Tel. 0034 650 952 721. 34 beds.
Open from April to October.
5€ per night. Closing hour: 22.00h
• **Albergue Nuestra Señora del Pilar.**
Pza. Morán Alonso. Tel. 0034 987 631 621.
72 beds. 5€ per night. Closing hour: 23.00h
• **Albergue Gaucelmo.** C/. Calvario, 4.
Tel. 0034 987 691 901. 46 beds.
Open from April to October.
Relies on voluntary donations.
Closing hour: 22.30h

Foncebadón
• **Albergue Domus Dei.** C/. Real.
No telephone. 18 beds.
Open from April to October.
Relies on voluntary donations.
Closing hour: 22.30h
• **Albergue Monte Irago.**
Tel. 0034 695 452 950. 35 beds. Open all year.
6€ per night. Closing hour: 22.00h
• **Albergue Convento de Foncebadón.**
C/. Real, s/n.
Tel. 0034 658 974 818. 30 beds.
Open from February to November.
7€ per night. Closing hour: 22.00h

STAGE 22
Manjarín
• **Refugio de Manjarín.**
No telephone. 50 beds. Open all year.
Relies on voluntary donations.
No closing hour.

El Acebo
• **Albergue Apóstol Santiago.**
Beside the church.
No telephone. 23 beds.
Open from April to October.
Relies on voluntary donations.
Closing hour: 22.30h

• **Albergue Mesón El Acebo.** C/. Real, 16.
Tel. 0034 987 695 074. 18 beds.
Open all year except for Christmas holidays.
5€ per night. Closing hour: 23.00h
• **Albergue La Taberna de José.** C/. Real, 19.
Tel. 0034 987 695 074. 14 beds.
Open all year except for Christmas holidays.
5€ per night. No closing hour.

Riego de Ambros
• **Albergue de Riego de Ambros.** C/. Real.
Tel. 0034 987 695 190. 30 beds.
Open from April to November.
5€ per night. Closing hour: 22.30h

Molinaseca
• **Albergue de Molinaseca.**
Av. Fraga Iribarne s/n.
Tel. 0034 987 453 077. 45 beds. Open all year.
5€ per night. Closing hour: 23.00h
• **Albergue Santa Marina.**
Av. Fraga Iribarne s/n.
Tel. 0034 615 302 390. 56 beds.
Open from March to November.
7€ per night. Closing hour: 23.00h

Ponferrada
• **Refugio de Ponferrada.** C/. Loma s/n.
Tel. 0034 987 413 381. 210 beds. Open all year.
Relies on voluntary donations.
Closing hour: 22.30h

STAGE 23
Cacabelos
• **Albergue de Cacabelos.** Pza. Santuario.
Tel. 0034 987 547 167. 70 beds.
Open from May to October.
6€ per night. Closing hour: 23.00h

Pieros
• **Albergue El Serbal y La Luna.**
C/ El Pozo, 15.
Tel. 0034 639 888 924. 19 beds. Open all year.
5€ per night. Closing hour: 21.00h

Villafranca del Bierzo
• **Albergue municipal Villafranca del Bierzo.**
Beside Iglesia de Santiago.
Tel. 0034 987 542 680. 62 beds.
Open from March to November.
6€ per night. Closing hour: 22.30h
• **Refugio Ave Fénix.** C/. Santiago, 10.
Tel. 0034 987 540 229. 80 beds.
www.albergueavefenix.com. Open all year.
5€ per night. Closing hour: 22.30h
• **Albergue de la Piedra.** C/. Espíritu Santo, 14.
Tel. 0034 987 540 260. 28 beds.
www.alberguedelapiedra.com.
Open from March to November.
Reservation required outside those months.
8€ per night. Closing hour: 22.30h

• Albergue Viña Femita. C/ Calvo Sotelo, 2.
Tel. 0034 987 542 490. 32 beds.
Open from mid-January to mid-December.
8€ per night. Closing hour: 23.00h

STAGE 24
Pereje
• Albergue de Pereje.
C/. Camino de Santiago s/n.
Tel. 0034 987 540 138. 30 beds. Open all year.
6€ per night. Closing hour: 22.00h

Trabadelo
• Albergue de Trabadelo.
C/. Camino de Santiago.
Tel. 0034 647 635 831. 36 beds.
Open from February to November.
6€ per night. Closing hour: 22.30h
• Albergue Crispeta.
C/. Camino de Santiago, 1.
Tel. 0034 620 329 386. 34 beds.
www.osarroxos.com. Open all year.
6€ per night. Closing hour: 23.00h

La Portela de Valcarce
• Albergue El Peregrino.
C/. Camino de Santiago, 5.
Tel. 0034 987 543 197. 28 beds.
www.laportela.com. Open all year.
8€ per night. Closing hour: 00.00h

Ambasmestas
• Albergue Das Ánimas. C/. Campo Bajo, 3.
Tel. 0034 691 048 626. 18 beds.
www.dasanimas.com.
Open from April to October.
5€ per night. Closing hour: 22.00h

Vega de Valcarce
• Albergue de Vega de Valcarce.
C/. Pandelo s/n.
Tel. 0034 657 097 954. 92 beds. Open all year.
5€ per night. No closing hour.
• Albergue Nuestra Señora Aparecida
do Brasil.
Ctra. Nacional 6, km 426.
Tel. 0034 987 543 045. 46 beds. Open all year.
7€ per night. Closing hour: 23.00h

Ruitelán
• Refugio Pequeño Potala. Ctra. A Coruña, 22.
Tel. 0034 987 561 322. 34 beds.
Open all year.
5€ per night. Closing hour: 23.00h

Las Herrerías
• Refugio en Herrerias.
Tel. 0034 654 353 940. 19 beds.
Open from April to October.
5€ per night. No closing hour.

La Faba
• Albergue Ultreia. Beside the church.
No telephone. 35 beds.
Open from April to October.
5€ per night. Closing hour: 22.00h

Laguna de Castilla
• Albergue La Escuela.
C/. Camino de Santiago.
Tel. 0034 987 684 786. 20 beds.
Open from April to October.
9€ per night. Closing hour: 23.00h

O Cebreiro
• Albergue de O Cebreiro.
Tel. 0034 660 396 809. 104 beds. Open all year.
5€ per night. Closing hour: 22.00h

STAGE 25
Hospital
• Albergue de Hospital da Condesa.
Tel. 0034 660 396 810. 20 beds. Open all year.
5€ per night. Closing hour: 22.00h

Alto do Poio
• Albergue Alto do Poio.
Tel. 0034 982 367 172. 16 beds. Open all year.
6€ per night. Closing hour: 23.00h

Fonfría
• Albergue A Reboleira.
C/. Camino de Santiago, 15.
Tel. 0034 982 181 271. 120 beds.
Open from March to November.
8€ per night. Closing hour: 23.00h

Biduedo
• Albergue Quiroga.
Tel. 0034 982 187 299. 16 beds. Open all year.
35€ per night for a double room.
No closing hour.

Triacastela
• Albergue de Triacastela.
Tel. 0034 982 548 087. 56 beds. Open all year.
5€ per night. Closing hour: 22.00h
• Albergue Complexo Xacobeo.
C/. Leoncio Cadórnigo, 12.
Tel. 0034 982 548 037. 48 beds.
www.complexoxacobeo.com.
Open all year.
9€ per night. No closing hour.
• Albergue Refugio del Oribio.
Av. Castilla, 20.
Tel. 0034 982 548 085. 27 beds.
Open all year.
9€ per night. Closing hour: 23.00h
• Albergue Aitzenea. Pza. Vista Alegre, 1.
Tel. 0034 982 548 076. 38 beds.
Open from April to October.
7€ per night. Closing hour: 23.00h

• **Albergue Berce do Caminho.**
C/. Camilo José Cela, 11.
Tel. 0034 982 548 127. 27 beds. Open all year.
7€ per night. Closing hour: 23.00h
• **Albergue A Horta de Abel.**
Rúa del Peregrino, 5.
Tel. 0034 608 080 556. 20 beds.
Open from April to mid-October.
9€ per night. Closes from 22.00 to 23.00h

STAGE 26
Lusío
• **Casa Forte de Lusío.**
Lusío is on the Samos route and lies between
San Cristovo do Real and Renche. It is some
400 metres off the Way and is signposted.
Tel. 0034 659 721 324. 60 beds. Open all year.
5€ per night. Closing hour: 22.00h

Samos
• **Monasterio de Samos.**
Monasterio de Samos, 1.
Tel. 0034 982 546 046. 90 beds.
Open all year. Relies on voluntary donations.
Closing hour: 22.30h
• **Casa de turismo vacacional**
Casiña de Madeira.
Beside Capilla de Ciprés.
Tel. 0034 653 824 546. 4 beds. Open all year.
36€ per night. No closing hour.
• **Albergue Val de Samos.**
Avenida Compostela, 16.
Tel. 0034 982 546 163. 48 beds.
Open from mid-April to November.
Outside those months reservations may be
made for groups.
11€ per night. Closing hour: 23.00h
• **Albergue A Cova do Frade.** C/ Salvador, 1
(opposite the Monasterio de Samos).
Tel. 0034 982 546 087. 20 beds.
Open all year except December and January.
9€ per night.
Closing hour: from 23.00 to 00.00h

Calvor
• **Refugio de los Peregrinos de Calvor.**
Old schoolhouses. From the roundabout,
the only building immediately visible.
Tel. 0034 660 396 812. 22 beds. Open all year.
5€ per night. Closing hour: 22.00h

San Mamede do Camiño
• **Albergue Privado Paloma y Leña.**
At Prado Novo, within the parish of
San Mamede do Camiño.
Tel. 0034 982 533 248. 32 beds.
Open from mid-February to late November.
10€ per night. No closing hour.

Sarria
• **Albergue de peregrinos de Sarria.**
C/. Mayor, 31.
Tel. 0034 660 396 813. 40 beds.
Open all year.
5€ per night. Closing hour: 23.00h
• **Albergue los Blasones.** C/. Mayor, 31.
Tel. 0034 600 512 565. 42 beds.
www.alberguelosblasones.com.
Open from March to November.
Outside those months, only groups with
prior reservation. Price: on enquiry.
Closing hour: 23.00h
• **Albergue Don Álvaro.** C/. Mayor, 10.
Tel. 0034 982 531 592. 40 beds.
www.alberguedonalvaro.com. Open all year.
9€ per night. Closing hour: 23.00h
• **Albergue A Pedra.** C/. Vigo de Sarria, 19.
Tel. 0034 982 530 130. 15 beds.
Open from March to November.
9€ per night. Closing hour: 23.00h
• **Albergue O Durmiñento.** C/. Mayor, 44.
Tel. 0034 982 531 099. 43 beds.
Open from March to December.
10€ per night. Closing hour: 23.00h
• **Albergue dos Oito Marabedís.**
C/. Conde de Lemos, 23.
Tel. 0034 629 461 770. 24 beds.
Open from May to October.
10€ per night. Closing hour: 23.00h
• **Albergue internacional Sarria.** C/. Mayor, 57.
Tel. 0034 982 535 109. 44 beds.
www.albergueinternacionalsarria.es.
Open all year.
10€ per night. Closing hour: 23.00h
• **Albergue Casa Peltre.** Escalinata da Fonte, 10
(beside the *peregrinoteca*).
Tel. 0034 606 226 067. 22 beds.
Open from March to October.
10€ per night. Closing hour: 22.30h
• **Albergue San Lázaro.** C/ San Lázaro, 7.
Tel. 0034 659 185 482. 30 beds.
Open from April to October.
10€ per night. Closing hour: 23.00h

Barbadelo
• **Albergue de Barbadelo.** Old schoolhouses.
Tel. 0034 660 396 814. 18 beds. Open all year.
5€ per night. Closing hour: 22.00h
• **Albergue A Casa de Carmen.**
San Silvestre Barbadelo, 3.
Tel. 0034 982 532 294. 30 beds. Open all year.
10€ per night. Closing hour: 23.00h
• **Albergue O Pombal.**
100 metres from the public hostel.
Tel. 0034 686 718 732. 8 beds.
Open from April to November.
10€ per night. Closing hour: 23.00h

STAGE 27
Morgade
This village lies between Brea and Ferreiros, after the stone marking the last 100 kilometres.
• Albergue Casa Morgade. Parish of A Pinza.
Tel. 0034 982 531 250. 16 beds.
Open from Holy Week to early November.
10€ per night. Closing hour: 22.30h

Ferreiros
• Albergue de Ferreiros. On the Way.
Tel. 0034 982 157 496. 22 beds. Open all year.
5€ per night. Closing hour: 22.00h

Mercadoiro
• Albergue Mercadoiro.
Aldea de Mercadoiro, 2.
Parroquia de Santiago de Laxe,
Concello de Paradela.
Tel. 0034 982 545 359. 36 beds.
Open from March to mid-November.
10€ per night. No closing hour.

Portomarín
• Albergue de Portomarín. Ctra. de Lugo.
Tel. 0034 982 545 143. 110 beds.
Open all year.
5€ per night. Closing hour: 22.00h
• Albergue O Mirador. C/. Peregrino, 27.
Tel. 0034 982 545 323. 29 beds.
www.omiradorportomarin.com. Open all year.
10€ per night. Closing hour: 23.00h
• Albergue Ferramenteiro. C/. Chantada, 3.
Tel. 0034 982 545 362. 120 beds.
Open depending on demand.
10€ per night. Closing hour: 23.00h
• Albergue El Caminante. C/. Sánchez Carro.
Tel. 0034 982 545 176. 46 beds.
Open from Holy Week to October.
10€ per night. Closing hour: 00.00h
• Albergue PortoSantiago. C/. Diputación, 8.
Tel. 0034 681 826 515. 14 beds.
www.albergueportosantiago.com.
Open all year.
10€ per night. Closing hour: 23.00h
• Albergue juvenil Benigno Quiroga.
Av. Sarria, 20.
Tel. 0034 982 545 022. 25 beds. Open all year.
Price: on enquiry. Closing hour: enquire.
• Albergue Manuel. C/ Rúa do Miño, 1.
Tel. 0034 982 545 385. 16 beds.
Open from April to October.
10€ per night. No closing hour.
Albergue Ultreia. C/ Diputación, 9.
Tel. 0034 982 545 067. 23 beds. Open all year.
10€ per night. Closing hour: 23.00h

Gonzar
• Albergue de Gonzar. On the Way.
Tel. 0034 982 157 840. 20 beds. Open all year.
5€ per night. Closing hour: 22.00h

• Albergue Casa García. C/. Gonzar, 3.
Tel. 0034 982 157 842. 40 beds. Open all year.
10€ per night. Closing hour: 23.00h

STAGE 28
Hospital de la Cruz
• Albergue Ventas de Narón.
Old schoolhouses.
Tel. 0034 982 545 232. 22 beds. Open all year.
5€ per night. Closing hour: 23.00h

Ventas de Narón
• Albergue Casa Molar. C/. Ventas, 4.
Tel. 0034 696 794 507. 22 beds. Open all year.
10€ per night. Closing hour: 23.00h
• Albergue O Cruceiro.
C/. Ventas de Narón, 6.
Tel. 0034 658 064 917. 26 beds. Open all year.
10€ per night. Closing hour: 23.00h

Ligonde
• Albergue de peregrinos Escuela de Ligonde.
Tel. 0034 679 816 061. 20 beds. Open all year.
6€ per night. No closing hour.
• Albergue Fuente del Peregrino.
Tel. 0034 687 550 527. 20 beds.
Open from June to September.
Relies on voluntary donations.
Closing hour: 22.00h

Airexe
• Albergue de Airexe.
Old schoolhouses.
Tel. 0034 982 153 483. 18 beds. Open all year.
5€ per night. Closing hour: 23.00h

Lestedo
• Albergue A Calzada.
The hostel is after Portos, on the left,
before arriving in the parish of Lestedo.
Tel. 0034 982 183 744. 10 beds.
Open from April to September.
10€ per night.
Closing hour: from 22.30 to 23.00h

Palas de Rei
• Albergue de Palas de Rei.
Ctra. Compostela, 19.
Tel. 0034 660 396 820. 60 beds. Open all year.
5€ per night. Closing hour: 23.00h
• Albergue Buen Camino.
C/. Peregrino, 3.
Tel. 0034 639 882 229. 41 beds.
www.alberguebuencamino.com.
Open from March to October.
10€ per night. Closing hour: 23.00h
• Albergue Mesón de Benito.
Rua da Paz, s/n.
Tel. 0034 636 834 065. 100 beds.
Open from Holy Week to mid-October.
10€ per night. Closing hour: 23.30h

• **Albergue Os Chacotes.**
C/ As Lagartas, s/n, at Os Chacotes sports grounds, 1 km from Palas de Rei.
Tel. 0034 607 481 536. 112 beds. Open all year.
5€ per night. Closing hour: 22.00h

San Xulián do Camiño
• **Albergue O Abrigadoiro.**
Tel. 0034 982 374 717. 18 beds.
Open from Holy Week to October.
12€ per night. Closing hour: 23.00h

Casanova
• **Albergue Casa Domingo.**
Pontecampaña-Mato.
Tel. 0034 982 163 226. 18 beds.
Open from April to October.
10€ per night. Closing hour: 23.00h
• **Albergue de Mato Casanova.**
Parroquia de Mato.
Tel. 0034 982 173 483. 20 beds. Open all year.
5€ per night. Closing hour: 23.00h

Vilar de Remonde
• **Albergue Turístico A Bolboreta.**
The village of Vilar de Remonde is 1.5 km off the Way. The turn-off, to the left, is in Casanova.
Tel. 0034 609 124 717. 26 beds. Open all year.
13€ per night with breakfast.
Closing hour: 23.00h

Melide
• **Albergue de Melide.** C/. San Antonio s/n.
Tel. 0034 660 396 822. 169 beds. Open all year.
5€ per night. Closing hour: 22.00h
• **Albergue O Apalpador.** C/ San Antonio, 23.
Tel. 0034 679 837 969. 30 beds. Open all year.
12€ per night. Closing hour: 23.00h

STAGE 29
Castañeda
• **Albergue Santiago.**
Tel. 0034 981 501 711. 6 beds. Open all year.
11€ per night. No closing hour.

Ribadiso da Baixo
• **Albergue de Ribadiso da Baixo.**
Tel. 0034 981 501 185. 70 beds. Open all year.
5€ per night. Closing hour: 23.00h

Arzúa
• **Albergue de Arzúa.** C/. Cima de Lugar, 6.
Tel. 0034 660 396 824. 48 beds. Open all year.
5€ per night. Closing hour: 23.00h
• **Albergue Ultreia.** C/. Lugo, 126.
Tel. 0034 981 500 471. 39 beds. Open all year.
10€ per night. Closing hour: 22.30h
• **Albergue Vía Láctea.** C/. José Antonio, 26.
Tel. 0034 981 500 581. 60 beds.
www.albergvialactea.com. Open all year.
10€ per night. Closing hour: 23.00h

• **Albergue Don Quijote.** On the Way.
Tel. 0034 981 500 139. 50 beds.
www.alberguedonquijote.com. Open all year.
10€ per night. Closing hour: 23.00h
• **Albergue Santiago Apóstol.**
Av. Lugo, 107.
Tel. 0034 981 508 132. 72 beds.
www.alberguesantiagoapostol.com.
Open all year.
12€ per night. Closing hour: 23.00h
• **Albergue da Fonte.** C/. Carme, 18.
Tel. 0034 659 999 496. 22 beds.
www.alberguedafonte.com.
Open from March to November.
10€ per night. Closing hour: 23.00h
• **Albergue Los Caminantes.**
Calle de Santiago, 14.
Tel. 0034 647 020 600. 35 beds.
Open from April to November.
10€ per night. Closing hour: 22.30h

Salceda
• **Albergue Pousada de Salceda.**
Main 547 road, km 75.
Tel. 0034 981 502 767. 14 beds. Open all year.
12€ per night. No closing hour.

Alto de Santa Irene
• **Albergue de Peregrinos Santa Irene.** Pino.
Tel. 0034 660 396 825. 36 beds. Open all year.
5€ per night. Closing hour: 22.00h
• **Albergue de peregrinos Santa Irene (private).** Pino.
Tel. 0034 981 511 000. 15 beds.
Open from April to October.
12€ per night. No closing hour.

Pedrouzo
• **Albergue de Arca do Pino.**
Tel. 0034 660 396 826. 120 beds. Open all year.
5€ per night. Closing hour: 23.00h
• **Albergue Porta de Santiago.** Av. Lugo, 11.
Tel. 0034 981 511 103. 60 beds.
www.portadesantiago.com. Open all year.
10€ per night. Closing hour: 23.00h
• **Albergue Edreira.** Rúa da Fonte, 19.
Tel. 0034 981 511 365. 56 beds.
Open from March to October.
November and December by reservation only.
12€ per night. Closing hour: 23.00h
• **Albergue O Burgo.** Avenida de Lugo, 47 (beside the service station).
Tel. 0034 630 404 138. 20 beds. Open all year.
10€ per night. Closing hour: 23.00h

STAGE 30
Monte do Gozo
• **Albergue del Monte do Gozo.**
Ctra. Aeropuerto, 2.
Tel. 0034 981 558 942. 370 beds. Open all year.
5€ per night. Closing hour: 22.00h

Santiago de Compostela
• Residencia de peregrinos San Lázaro.
C/. San Lázaro s/n.
Tel. 0034 981 571 488. 80 beds. Open all year.
10€ per night. No closing hour.
• Albergue Seminario Menor La Asunción.
C/. Belvís s/n.
Tel. 0034 881 031 768. 199 beds.
Open from March to November.
12€ per night. Closing hour: 23.00h
• Albergue Acuario. C/. San Lázaro, 2.
Tel. 0034 981 575 438. 52 beds.
Open from March to November.
10€ per night. Closing hour: 00.00h
• Albergue Santo Santiago. Rúa do Valiño, 3.
Tel. 0034 657 402 403. 30 beds. Open all year.
13€ per night. Closing hour: 23.30h
• Albergue Mundoalbergue.
C/San Clemente, 26.
Tel. 0034 696 448 737. 34 beds. Open all year.
16€ per night. Closing hour: 23.00h
• Albergue O Fogar de Teodomiro.
Plaza de Algalia de Arriba, 3
(a street leading onto Plaza Cervantes).
Tel. 0034 981 582 920. 20 beds. Open all year.
18€ per night. Closing hour: 20.00h
• Albergue de peregrinos Jaime García
Rodríguez. Rúa de Moscova, s/n.
Tel. 0034 981 587 324. 176 beds.
Open from April.
6€ per night. Closing hour: 00.00h

ON TO FINISTERRE, STAGE 31
Logrosa
• Albergue turístico de Logrosa. Logrosa, Nº 6.
At Chancela (the last town before Negreira)
take the turn-off to Logrosa. The hostel is
700 m from that turn-off.
Tel. 0034 981 885 820. 20 beds. Open all year.
15€ per night. Closing hour: enquire.

Negreira
• Albergue de Negreira. C/. Patrocinio s/n.
Tel. 0034 664 081 498. 20 beds. Open all year.
5€ per night. Closing hour: 22.00h
• Albergue turístico San José.
Rúa de Castelao, 20 bajo.
Tel. 0034 881 976 934. 50 beds.
Open from March to late November.
12€ per night. Closing hour: 22.30h
• Albergue Lua. Avenida de Santiago, 22.
Tel. 0034 629 926 802. 40 beds.
Open from March to October.
9€ per night. Closing hour: 22.00h

ON TO FINISTERRE, STAGE 32
Vilaserío
• Albergue de Vilaserío. Old schoolhouses.
No telephone. 20 beds. Open all year.

Relies on voluntary donations. No closing hour.
• Albergue O Rueiro. Vilaserío, s/n.
Tel. 0034 981 893 561. 30 beds. Open all year.
12€ per night. No closing hour.

Maroñas
• Albergue Antelo. On the Way.
Tel. 0034 981 852 897. 10 beds.
Enquire as to opening months.
10€ per night. Closing hour: 23.00h

Olveiroa
• Albergue de Olveiroa.
Tel. 0034 658 045 248. 34 beds. Open all year.
5€ per night. Closing hour: 23.00h

ON TO FINISTERRE, STAGE 33
Dumbría
This village is 9 km after Olveiroa,
on the road from Hospital to Muxia.
• Albergue de Peregrinos de Dumbría.
Beside the football pitch.
Tel. 0034 981 744 001 (Town Hall). 26 beds.
Open all year.
5€ per night. Closing hour: 22.00h

Cée
• Albergue O Camiño das Estrelas. Avenida
Finisterre, 78.
Tel. 0034 981 747 575. 30 beds. Open all year.
12€ per night. Closing hour: 23.00h
• Albergue O Bordón. Camiños Chans.
Tel. 0034 981 746 574. 24 beds. Open all year.
12€ per night. Closing hour: 23.30h

Corcubión
• Albergue San Roque. On the Way.
Tel. 0034 981 745 400. 20 beds. Open all year.

ON TO FINISTERRE, STAGE 34
Fisterra
• Albergue de Fisterra. C/. Real, 1.
Tel. 0034 981 740 781. 36 beds. Open all year.
5€ per night. Closing hour: 22.00h
• Albergue de Paz. C/. Víctor Cardalda, 11.
Tel. 0034 981 740 332. 30 beds. Open all year.
10€ per night. No closing hour.
• Albergue do Sol. C/ Atalaya, 7.
Tel. 0034 981 740 655. 29 beds. Open all year.
10€ per night. Closing hour: 23.00h
(although always open in practice).
• Albergue Finistellae. C/ Manuel Lago Pais, 7.
Tel. 0034 661 493 505. 20 beds. Open all year.
10€ per night. Closing hour: 22.30h
• Albergue O Encontro. Calle del campo.
Tel. 0034 696 503 363. 5 beds. Open all year.
15€ per night. Closing hour: 23.00h

Index of place names

The Official Guides to all o

Cotswold Way
Anthony Burton

100 miles of quintessentially
English landscape

ISBN 978 1 84513 785 4

Cleveland Way
Ian Sampson

Over 100 miles of magnificent
walking on the North York Moors

ISBN 978 1 84513 781 6

Pennine Way
Damian Hall

The whole of England's toughest
National Trail

ISBN 978 1 84513 718 2

Yorkshire Wolds Way
Roger Ratcliffe

A superbly tranquil walk through the
unspoilt chalk hills of East Yorkshire

ISBN 978 1 84513 643 7

Pembrokeshire Coast Path
Brian John

180 miles of clifftop, beach and cove
around the magnificent Welsh coast

ISBN 978 1 84513 602 4

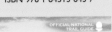

South Downs Way
Paul Millmore

100 miles of glorious chalk downland
for the walker, cyclist and horse rider

ISBN 978 1 84513 565 2

Hadrian's Wall Path
Anthony Burton

Follow the Roman Wall
from coast to coast

ISBN 978 1 84513 567 6

The Ridgeway
Anthony Burton

87 miles of downland walking
from Wiltshire to the Chilterns

ISBN 978 1 84513 638 3

North Downs Way
Colin Saunders

Follow the chalk ridge across South-East
England all the way to the sea

ISBN 978 1 84513 677 2

Britain's National Trails

Thames Path
in the Country
David Sharp and Tony Gowers
From the source to Hampton Court

ISBN 978 1 84513 717 5

Thames Path
in London
Phoebe Clapham
From Hampton Court to Crayford Ness:
50 miles of historic riverside walk

ISBN 978 1 84513 706 9

Peddars Way and
Norfolk Coast Path
Bruce Robinson with Mike Robinson
90 miles from Breckland to
salt marsh and sea cliffs

ISBN 978 1 84513 784 7

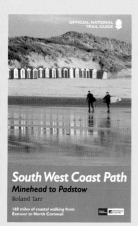

South West Coast Path
Minehead to Padstow
Roland Tarr
160 miles of coastal walking from
Exmoor to North Cornwall

ISBN 978 1 84513 640 6

South West Coast Path
Padstow to Falmouth
John Macadam
From golden beaches to rugged coves
around Britain's southernmost tip

ISBN 978 1 84513 641 3

Offa's Dyke Path
SOUTH: Chepstow to Knighton
Ernie and Kathy Kay and Mark Richards
Follow the ancient earthwork up the Wye
Valley and alongside the Black Mountains

ISBN 978 1 84513 561 4

South West Coast Path
Falmouth to Exmouth
Brian Le Messurier
172 miles of dramatic coves, cliffs and
beaches from Cornwall to Devon

ISBN 978 1 84513 564 5

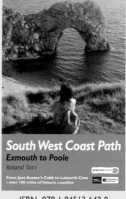

South West Coast Path
Exmouth to Poole
Roland Tarr
From Jane Austen's Cobb to Lulworth Cove
– over 100 miles of historic coastline

ISBN 978 1 84513 642 0

NATIONAL TRAIL GUIDES
OFFA'S DYKE PATH NORTH
Knighton to Prestatyn
Ernie and Kathy Kay and Mark Richards
100 miles of walking through the
beautiful Welsh marches

ISBN 978 1 84513 312 2

PENNINE BRIDLEWAY
Derbyshire to the
South Pennines
Sue Viccars

ISBN 1 85410 957 X

Definitive guides to other popular long-distance walks published by

Aurum

The Capital Ring
Colin Saunders

78 miles of green corridor
encircling inner London

ISBN 978 1 84513 786 1

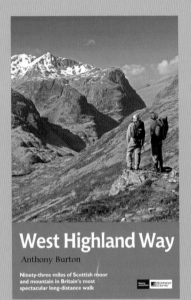

West Highland Way
Anthony Burton

Ninety-three miles of Scottish moor
and mountain in Britain's most
spectacular long-distance walk

ISBN 978 1 84513 569 0

The London Loop
David Sharp

The walker's M25 ~ over 140 miles of
footpaths in London's secret countryside

ISBN 978 1 84513 787 8

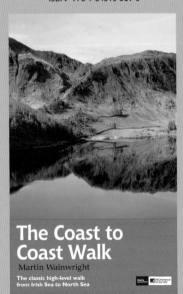

The Coast to Coast Walk
Martin Wainwright

The classic high-level walk
from Irish Sea to North Sea

ISBN 978 1 84513 560 7